8/09/2011 (10T)

DEC 0 5 2008

Let's Talk About Pep

Let's Talk About Pep

SANDY "PEPA" DENTON

with Karen Hunter

Pocket Books
New York   London   Toronto   Sydney

Pocket Books
A Division of Simon & Schuster, Inc.
1230 Avenue of the Americas
New York, NY 10020

First MTV Books/Pocket Books hardcover edition August 2008

POCKET and colophon are registered trademarks of Simon & Schuster, Inc.

For information about special discounts for bulk purchases, please contact Simon & Schuster Special Sales at 1-800-456-6798 or business@simonandschuster.com.

Designed by Mary Austin Speaker

Manufactured in the United States of America

10   9   8   7   6   5   4   3   2   1

Library of Congress Cataloging-in-Publication Data
Denton, Sandra.
  Let's talk about Pep / Sandy "Pepa" Denton with Karen Hunter.—1st
MTV Books/Pocket Books hardcover ed.
      p. cm.
  1. Denton, Sandra, 1969- 2. Rap musicians—United States—Biography.
I. Hunter, Karen. II. Title.
  ML420.D455A3 2008
  782.421649092—dc22
  [B]
                                        2008028402
ISBN-13: 978-1-4165-5141-6
ISBN-10:   1-4165-5141-7

To my father and my mother.

I also want to dedicate this book to the many women who think they're all alone in their pain. You can get through it. Trust me. And know you are worthy.

Acknowledgments

I WANT TO THANK MY children, Tyran and Egypt, for bringing joy into my life and giving mommy space to grow and be able to share my story. To Tee Tee (Tahira), my niece and my girl, who also brings so much light into my life. Stay up!

And to the entire Denton family, my backbone and my heart. While there are too many of you to name, you all know who are and know that I love you all.

My girl, Salt (Cheryl Wray), who has been telling me for years, "You need to write a book! You need to put all of that into a book!" Well, here it is. Thank you, Cheryl, for always pushing me to do this and for always encouraging me to follow my dreams.

Karen Hunter, thank you for making this journey so much easier than it would have been, for asking the right questions and getting me to go deeper than I wanted to. You were a blessing.

Thank you, Charles Suitt, for making that phone call and helping to make this happen.

Acknowledgments

I want to thank Pocket Books, Simon & Schuster, and MTV Books for having the vision to publish my story.

To my editor, Lauren McKenna, thank you for pushing for more and getting it. And thank you for your patience. Also to Brigitte Smith, for staying on top of the details.

To all of the men I've ever been with, thank you for showing me all of the things I need to avoid in my future. Also thank you for giving me the valuable experience to be able to share and help others to learn from my story.

And last but not least, to the one Man who has never let me down—God. Thank God for seeing me through all of my trials and allowing me to be the woman I am today.

Contents

Contents

Introduction

by Queen Latifah

I REMEMBER THE FIRST TIME I ever heard Salt-N-Pepa. It was at the Latin Quarters in New York. Actually, I had heard them a few times on the radio. But I really grew to appreciate them and really take notice of them in the clubs. When I was fifteen, I used to sneak to New York and hang out at the hip-hop spots. I was totally into it and when that one song came on, I fell in love.

It was *My Mic Sounds Nice*. And the first thing that caught my attention was the way they spit their lyrics: *My mic sounds nice, check one.*

I was like, "Whoa, who is that?!"

The chords were so hot; the sample was so dope. It was edgy. It was raw. They had this go-go rhythm working and it was all so different from everything else I was hearing in hip-hop. And when that song came on in the Latin Quarters everybody hit the floor and the club went crazy. From the hardest dudes to the softest girls, everybody would be rocking to that record.

Salt-N-Pepa didn't just come onto the scene as a pop sensation. They had the respect of the streets, of the clubs, of the people. And they paved the way for me to do my thing.

There weren't many females on the mic when I was growing up. There was no MC Lyte or Lil' Kim or Missy. There was Roxanne Shanté and Sweet T and DJ Jazzy Joyce. Salt-N-Pepa took the female rap game to a whole other level.

They were hard, but soft. They were cute and had their own style. They were trendsetters. And they were real. They were the queens from Queens who helped make it possible for this queen to become Queen Latifah.

The first time I met Pep was at a party. It was actually a party for Salt-N-Pepa. I had met them before in passing, but on this night, I actually got to hang out with them. And I remember it clearly. Both she and Salt were very down to earth, but Sandy was just crazy fun.

Later when she got with Old Boy, we started to really hang out and I got to see another side of Sandy Denton. Of course, there was the fun side. Hanging out with her, there was definitely going to be some fun. There might be magic tricks or a spades game that could break out at any time. She would even make up some stuff. There was a talk show host named Jenny Jones. Well, Pep came up with Jeni-fa Jones and we would act out the ghetto version of the show. If you hung out with Pep, you were going to laugh.

But I also got to see the other side. Not that she ever showed that willingly. If you hung around Pep, she would always have a smile on her face. But if you slowed her down long enough, you might get see that there was something more there, something behind the laughter and the smile. I got to see some of that, too. We were family. She is family!

She's been through a lot. We used to talk about it. I had some of the same experiences she had—and unfortunately, these are stories that too many women share.

Getting to know Sandy and seeing her spirit, I can see how some people who aren't right might try to take advantage of her kindness and her spirit. Pep is so sweet and so cool. And I know that some of the times between her and Old Boy were pretty rocky. But she got through them. She's a survivor. She's an inspiration in many ways.

I'm extremely proud of the woman she has become. I got to see some of the before—watching her deal with some of the demons and that's not easy. As someone who has had to deal with some of those very issues myself, I know it's not easy. And it's especially hard when you're in the public eye.

I know it's not easy to confront it. And a lot of times those demons haunt you and they affect your relationships and your life. I know this firsthand, too

It's nice to see Sandy confront some of her issues, take them on, and talk about them. It's also nice to see her reconcile with Cheryl. It's good to see them back together—not as a group but as girls.

I missed Salt-N-Pepa. And I'm glad they have come full circle and that they slowed down long enough to get back to being just Sandy and Cheryl instead of jumping on the bandwagon back into that crazy life of hip hop artists.

I'm glad that Sandy is writing this book and getting it all out. I know her story may surprise a few people, but I hope that it helps many more. I'm glad she's writing this book so that people can see the layers, and get to see the phases she's been through, and also get to see some of what so many of us have enjoyed and loved over the years.

Let me introduce you all to my girl, my sister, Sandra Denton. But you can call her Pep.

Expression

MOST OF YOU KNOW ME as Pep, or Pepa, the fun-loving half of Salt-N-Pepa. I am the party girl, the one who is down for whatever. I'm the one that's at a party until the credits roll. But behind the laughs and the smiles is a whole lot of pain.

When I started writing this book, I hadn't reconciled with Cheryl (aka Salt). And a lot of this book was going to be about how pissed off I was that she left me for dead, when she walked away from Salt-N-Pepa, with no notice.

"I'm out!" she told me on my cell phone one afternoon out of the blue. "I'm tired of being joined at your hip."

That call turned my life inside out. I mean, I had no identity outside of Salt-N-Pepa. For fifteen years I was part of something that produced gold and platinum records, made millions of dollars for a whole lot of people, and had me traveling around the world, hanging with legends, dignitaries, and even a prince. I learned really quickly that without Salt, there was no Pepa. No one wanted just Pepa. I couldn't tour by myself. I felt as if Cheryl had snatched my identity, had stripped me of everything I had worked for. I didn't know how to do anything else. I didn't *want* to do anything else. And now I was forced to find something else to do with the rest of my life—against my will.

And it wasn't about the money. We'd signed a pretty nice deal before she decided to leave. But once again, I didn't have any say or any control over what was happening to me. It was as if I were seven and someone were doing something to me that I didn't want all over again. And I rebelled. I acted out. I did some crazy things—most of them self-destructive. I lost a lot of money; I surrounded myself with all the wrong people. In my mind, I was getting back at Cheryl. But I know now, I was only hurting myself.

As I started thinking about my life in preparation for this book, I discovered some things that I hadn't realized. One is, it's important to talk. It's important to get stuff off your chest. It's important to let it all out. The other thing is, no one can do anything to you unless you allow him to. You have control over you.

Control—losing it, giving it to others, not having it—has been one of the things haunting me my entire life.

I realized that my whole life has been about allowing situations and people to happen to me. I didn't say anything when my friend's grandfather molested me when I was seven. I was reluctant to say anything when my sister's boyfriend violated me. I didn't say anything when I was almost gang-raped in my neighborhood. I didn't say anything when I was getting beaten by my man—several different men. I let people steal from me, take things from me—including my career.

But now is my time to speak up. I'm saying something.

Before the start of the last year, I made a resolution. Actually, I made a promise to myself to be on time. I had been watching an episode of our reality show, *The Salt-N-Pepa Show* on VH-1, and I hated what I saw. It's funny, when you're just living your life, you don't notice things about yourself—even when people are telling you about yourself over and over. You just do what you do. But when you get to see yourself (and few of us get that opportunity) is when you really get to *see* yourself.

I've been late my whole life. It's been a running joke. I know it's bad. I can have an appointment at one o'clock and I'll just be leaving my house at one thirty. And the whole time, I am mad at myself. I scream, "Why do you do this?!" It's so stressful to always be late. I never wanted to be late, and I definitely wasn't late to hurt anyone. I couldn't explain why I was always late until now.

Cheryl and I had an episode where we had to go on a counseling retreat with Iyanla VanZandt. We were supposed to work through our differences in this remote area in the mountains with no phones, no outside distractions—just Cheryl and me talking it out. Well, there was so much drama with that, Ms. VanZandt and I didn't quite see eye to eye.

What do you mean, no phone?! You must be crazy!

But after we got over our initial issues, one thing that came out of the weekend was why I'm always late.

"So how old were you when it happened?" Ms. VanZandt said to me.

I looked at her, puzzled. "What are you talking about?"

"How old were you when you were first molested?"

What is she, psychic? How did she know? I was completely shocked. I paused before I answered her.

"I was seven."

"I was ten," she said. "Being late is a classic trait of someone who was molested at a young age. It's like their way of having some sort of control. It's one way of having power."

It made a lot of sense. I started thinking back to all of the things that had happened to me, and I could see a pattern, and I could also see where I tried to find my power or find my control in other areas. I also saw that I seemed to keep being attracted to men who would take from me, abuse me, and try to make me powerless. It was almost a sickness. How did I keep ending up with the same kind of man?

I finally decided to break the cycle, not just for myself, but also for my children, especially my little girl. She needed to have a mommy who was strong and who made good decisions and good choices.

My first good choice was to swear off relationships. I decided that until I met a man who could give me what I needed (instead of me trying to fix him and be there for him), I would be alone. In October of 2005, I decided I would be celibate.

At the time of this book, I am still celibate. It has been both the best thing I have ever done for myself and also one of the toughest. I mean, when you have been sexual most of your life, it's hard to just not do it anymore. Being celibate, I have learned that sex for me was a crutch most of the time.

I can honestly say I don't think I've ever been in love. I mean in *love* love—the kind of fairy-tale love that makes you want to be a better person, that makes you feel good from the inside out. The kind of love that when you think about that person, your whole world lights up. I really want to know what that feels like because I never have. And I am willing to wait for it. I know now that I deserve that. I deserve to have the best in my life.

I didn't always feel that way. But I do now.

CHAPTER ONE

The Chameleon's Curse

I WAS BORN IN JAMAICA. My earliest memories are of being on my grandmother's farm in St. Elizabeth's, which was considered the cush-cush or upper-class section of Jamaica, between Negril and Kingston. We lived in what they called the country, and I just remember running free and not having a care in the world. I didn't come to the States until I was about six. That's when life became complicated.

I was the youngest of eight. The baby. My mother said I was the cutest baby she had ever seen. When I six months old, she entered me in this contest to be the face of O-Lac's, which was Jamaica's version of Gerber baby food. They were looking for a fat, healthy baby, and I won the contest. I was the face—this smiling, fat, tooth-less baby—on O-Lac's for years. I guess I was destined for stardom.

My parents moved to the United States when I was three. One by one, each of my sisters left, too. I know that my father had a government job in Jamaica. I don't know what happened with it. I just remember talk of "opportunity" and "education" in America.

In Jamaica, you had to pay for education after primary school. And getting an education was big in my family. So maybe that's why they left. I never asked. You didn't ask questions when I was growing up. My family was traditional, and kids didn't ask adults questions, you just accepted things—whatever those things were.

I ended up being in Jamaica with my grandmother and one of my older sisters. My parents would come back from time to time, but I was there for a couple of years before they finally moved me to the States, too.

I loved my family, but I never quite fit in with them. I was always a little bit different. My sister Dawn was the rebel, the black sheep. I watched how she used to get beatings—I mean real beatings, not some little old spankings—and I didn't want any of that. My parents, mostly my father, tried to beat the rebellion out of Dawn. It didn't work, though. It might have made her more rebellious.

By the time I got to the States, she was hanging out with the wrong crowds, staying out way beyond the curfew and trying to sneak in the house and getting caught. She used to steal my father's gun. She would fight. And eventually she turned to drugs. But that was my girl! I looked up to Dawn. I just didn't want to suffer any of those beatings, so I was a "good girl." I did what I was told—as far as they knew—and I stayed out of trouble. But I was always a little different.

When I was on that farm in Jamaica, I would get into all kinds of trouble. One day I remember I got ahold of a machete. I was only like five years old. Don't ask me how I got it or where I got it from, but I had this machete and a bucket. I went around the farm looking for lizards or chameleons. They had all kinds of creatures on this farm, but there were a lot of chameleons. I was fascinated by them, watching them go to a green plant and turn green, then to the ground and turn brown. I walked around looking for them, and I would chop them in half and throw them into my bucket.

By the end of the day, I had a bucket full of chopped-up lizards. My sister came out and saw what I was doing and she scared the hell out of me.

"What is that you're doing?!" she screamed. "Dem lizards gwon ride ya."

She was telling me that the lizards were going to haunt me. That my doing that had unleashed some kind of curse.

"Dem gwon ride ya!" my sister kept saying in her Jamaican patois.

Well, they did ride me. As I got older, a lot of my friends would tell me, "You're such a chameleon."

It was true. I was real good at blending in. I was good at taking on whatever was around me. If I hung out with thugs, I would be a thug. If I hung out with a prince, it was nothing for me to become royalty. My ability to fit in has been a blessing, but also a curse.

The very thing that got me into Salt-N-Pepa—going with the flow and doing what I was told—was the same thing that got me in a lot of bad situations. Being a chameleon or just going with whatever wasn't good for me. It allowed me to put up with things I shouldn't have put up with. It allowed me to be with people I should not have been with because I wasn't able to just be myself and say no or walk away. It never let me ask, "What do I want out of life?" It never allowed me to really think about me and my needs first.

I wanted to fit in. I wanted to be accepted. I wanted people to like me.

CHAPTER TWO

Coming to America

IT'S EASY TO GET LOST in a big family—especially as the youngest. I have six sisters and a brother. And they all had their roles in the family long before I came along.

There's my brother, Bully, who was the only boy. I didn't really get too tight with him because he was a boy and was so much older. He was out of the house by the time I came from Jamaica. I can't tell you exactly how old Bully is—actually, I'm sketchy on the ages of most of my siblings. You see, my mom was really big on not telling her age. So she used to get on all of us kids about telling our age. Because if you knew how old we were, you could probably figure out how old she is. And she wasn't having that.

To this day, I don't know how old my mother is because she

refuses to tell anyone. She won't even let her grandchildren call her grandma. If they even try, she will tell them, "Watch your mouth!" And she means it.

So I grew up in this kind of Hollywood family where everybody lied about his or her age.

I know Bully and Fay are the oldest, but I don't know who is older nor exactly how old either one is. I just learned never to ask. Fay is a lot like my mom. She likes to have a good time and to party. She's a lot of fun. She lives in Florida and has her own business. Then there's Jean, the bossy one. If you tried to go into her room, she would yell, "Get out!" But she was also the sister who used to take me to the circus, to the Ice Capades, and to Broadway plays when I was little.

I'm not really tight with Fiona, who is next in age. She had moved out and on with her life by the time I came into the picture. She was always into her own thing. She and Patsy were tight. Patsy is the adventurer in the family—not like me (who will try just about anything on a dare). Patsy *really* loves the outdoors—camping, hiking, nature, the woods, that kind of thing. If you're hanging with Patsy, she will have you doing outdoor activities or going to a science museum or a cave or something. And she will be feeding you something organic—some vegetarian lasagna. You're definitely going to eat your vegetables hanging with Patsy. She even grows her own in her garden.

Then there's Bev. She's the lawyer and the family organizer. She plans all of the trips (we try to take about two a year as a family), and all of the dinners for everybody's birthday. That's Bev's thing.

Then there is Dawn. The rebel. My protector.

Those are the Dentons. All of them moved to the States before I did. As I mentioned, I spent my first six years on a farm in

Jamaica with my grandmother while my family settled into life in the States. Both of my parents were strict and demanding—especially my father. He didn't take any crap and he expected the best from all of us.

"That's what Dentons do," he would say when one of my sisters brought home straight A's. And they all did. The Dentons made the honor roll. The Dentons worked hard. My parents' hard work allowed them to give us a pretty good life. I don't remember ever wanting for much growing up. Some of it had to do with having older siblings who also worked and would spoil me. Yes, I was the baby.

Moving to the United States was a culture shock for me. I went from this rural farm in Jamaica to the big city. We lived in Jamaica, Queens, of all places. My parents had the biggest house on Anderson Road—and we needed every bit of that space. Our house was like a boardinghouse. Any relative or friend who didn't have a place to stay, stayed with us. There were my six sisters, me, my mother and father, and whoever else needed a place to stay.

We used to play musical rooms in my house. I started out on the second floor with four of my sisters. But by the time I was eight, I was in the attic with my sister Dawn. My father had converted our basement into two bedrooms, and people were living down there.

Our house, including the attic, had four floors. And the house was always noisy. You could get lost in that house for days and no one would notice you because there was always something going on. Our house was alive.

My mother loved to party. That's probably where I got it from. My mom was always glamorous and fly, and she loved having people over and entertaining. She is quite a character. She would tell people about themselves in a minute (and she still does!). People are afraid of my mother's mouth. But you better not say anything to her.

My mom worked hard and partied hard. On the weekends our house was turned into a nightclub. She would host house parties where she and my dad would sell liquor and dinners, and there would be reggae and R&B blasting. The house would be rocking. It started off small with just a few friends and family members, then as word spread, people from the neighborhood would come and bring friends. Every week the party would be bigger and bigger.

I used to love it. To see all of those people laughing and dancing and having fun was a thrill. I would sneak downstairs and just watch. I couldn't wait for the day that I could be right there in the mix. I couldn't wait until I was grown.

I was the baby. And was always treated like the baby. Children were to be seen and not heard. My parents were from the old school. So I kept quiet and out of the way. That's how I was raised. I was always respectful—even to my sisters. Even Dawn, who was about six years older than I am, got respect. I looked up to her. My older sisters always took care of me, and I just naturally treated them with respect.

My sisters were more like my aunts, and many of them acted as if they were my mother (a couple of them had children around my age). I was as respectful with them as I was with my parents. If they told me to do something, I was mindful and would do it and wouldn't talk back to them. I never argued. To this day, they get that respect. My friends think it's weird how I treat my sisters, but that's how our family is.

I was like a chameleon even in my own house. I just tried to blend in, not make any waves, not cause any trouble.

That's not to say that I didn't get into any trouble. Before our basement was converted into bedrooms, I used to spend a lot of time down there playing by myself. I found some matches, and just like that time back on that farm in Jamaica, I guess I was bored and fascinated. I had seen quite a few people light a cigarette with these matches, and I wanted to figure out how to do it.

So there I was striking away. I would light one, then just toss it to the floor, afraid of burning my fingers. A bunch of blankets were in the corner of the basement, and I was lighting these matches and a couple of them landed on the blankets. The next thing I knew, the blankets caught on fire. I panicked and ran. Thank God the whole house didn't catch on fire and someone came and put it out before it got out of control.

I ran and got a bunch of toilet paper and put it in my pants. I just knew I was going to get a beating. My mother looked at me, and I must have looked so pitiful that she said, "I'm not even going to beat you." I couldn't believe it.

My mother was a beater. She beat everyone. My father didn't beat us often, but when he did, it was bad. I never wanted to do anything to get a beating from either of them, especially my father. My father would beat my sisters, my cousins. Whatever kid that was in the house and didn't behave got a beating. And he would beat you with anything—extension cord, belt, switch, paddle.

That was love in my home. No one ever said, "I love you." That just wasn't the way my parents were. There were no hugs and kisses. There was a lot of discipline and high standards. And I grew up thinking that everyone's household was like that.

When I got older and saw how other people interacted with their parents and heard their parents say, "I love you," I thought it was the strangest thing. Cheryl used to tease me a lot. She came from one of those "I love you" households. And she used to try to get me to be affectionate. She would say, "Give me a hug!" just to mess with me because she knew that would make me uncomfortable. I guess Cheryl broke me down. Either that or I just got used to it. I liked how it made me feel, too.

To this day, I'm one of the most affectionate people you will meet—especially with my kids. Not a day goes by that I don't tell my son and daughter that I love them, and they tell me that, too. It's just how we are. That's my rule. And my nieces and nephews gravitate toward me because they know Aunt Sandy will love them up.

But I understand my parents now. That's not how they were raised. Where they came from, showing affection just wasn't done. I didn't know better when I was younger, I just thought that was how people were.

My mother was funny, though. She had a funny way about her but I knew she loved us. She just had a different way of showing it.

I can't imagine raising so many kids and keeping it all together and still wanting a certain kind of life. I know she sacrificed a lot to have us. My mom is a dynamic woman.

She used to tell us all the time that if she didn't have us children, she would have been a politician or something. She had big dreams. She was really good at laying down the law and keeping the peace—by any means necessary. My mom was the politician in our home—solving all problems, keeping everyone together, and taking care of the household. And she was the neighborhood politician, throwing parties and being the life of the party. People loved being around my mother—even with her mouth.

As I said, we had a huge house. And on the weekends, the living room was turned into Club Denton. All of the furniture was moved out, and the food, liquor, and music were flowing with people wall to wall.

These parties were the place where everyone wanted to be. But one weekend it all got out of hand. I don't know exactly what happened. But someone couldn't get in or started some trouble and got into an argument and was escorted out of our house. He came back with a gun. I heard this *pop, pop, pop.* Windows shattered and people hit the floor. My sister Jean saw me walking around in a daze not quite understanding everything and she yelled at me, "Down! Down!"

I got down and a man fell right next to me. He was bleeding. Several people were bleeding and moaning and screaming. I was in shock. There was all this commotion. I wasn't crying. I wasn't hysterical. My mother was calm, too, when the shooting was over. Like a true politician, she knew how to make everybody feel as if everything was okay. When the bullets stopped flying, she got everybody up and out of the house calmly. She got that house cleaned up, the windows boarded, and by Monday it was as if nothing had happened. And nobody talked about it.

My mother taught me that things happen in life, but you have to pick up the pieces and keep on moving.

CHAPTER THREE

"And You Better Not Tell!"

"STOP! IT HURTS. I WANT to go." I was squirming and wiggling and trying to get away. But he was so strong, too strong. He had his hands all over me—in my panties, rubbing my little chest. He was rubbing my body against him. I could smell his breath and I wanted to throw up.

The only thing that made him stop was the door. His grandson had returned from the errand he was sent on. The man released me long enough for me to run. I ran out of the door and kept running until I got home. And I never went back.

Anthony was my friend who lived up the street. My family lived on the corner of Sidway and Anderson, and Anthony lived a few houses away on Sidway.

We were both seven. I called him my boyfriend. We would

play together every day. Mostly, he would come to my house. I played at his house a few times, too. On this day we had been playing on the front porch of his house when his grandfather called him. Anthony's parents weren't home.

"Anthony! I need you to go to store for me."

I was all prepared to go with Anthony. Maybe I could get some free candy out of it. But as I was about to leave, Anthony's grandfather called me to him.

"I want you to stay here with me."

Again, I was raised in an old-school household. Children always obeyed adults—no matter what. That's just how we were raised. I remember Anthony looking back at me kind of puzzled, and I looked at him funny, too. I knew something wasn't right.

His grandfather told me to come sit with him on the couch. I hesitated.

"Come on over here, girl. I don't bite."

I figured he couldn't bite because he didn't have a tooth in his head. But he was grinning at me as if he was so happy.

"Come sit over here." He patted the couch next to him. "Don't worry."

I needed to worry. I was alone with this man, this old man. But being obedient, I nervously walked over and sat next to him. Before I could sit down, he grabbed me and put me on his lap. He was poking me with his fingers and got inside my pants, and then I felt him poking around the legs of my panties. He was trying to stick his fingers inside me. I just remember it hurting.

"Ow!" I said. "Stop!"

But he was ignoring me. I think back now and I say to myself, "Wow, this old man was really going for it with a little girl."

"That hurts; I want to go," I said, squirming around, trying to get free.

"Shh," he said in my ear. "And you better not tell anybody!"

Where was Anthony! Why wasn't he back yet?

It seemed as if he were gone forever. Not only was his grandfather hurting me, but I couldn't understand *why* he was doing this to me.

And you better not tell!

Finally, I heard the front door. Anthony was back and his grandfather loosened his grip long enough for me to get away from him. I ran for the door and kept running until I got to my house. I was confused, hurt, and scared. I didn't know what I should do, but I remembered those words: *And you better not tell!*

I didn't tell. I was always taught to respect and mind my elders. And while I knew inside what Anthony's grandfather had done to me was wrong, I couldn't tell anyone. I was also embarrassed and may have felt that it was my fault. I don't know. I knew playing with Anthony was over. It wasn't his fault, but I didn't want to be around him anymore. I didn't want to be reminded of what his grandfather had done. So I found some new friends or I played by myself.

This thing that happened so many years ago definitely messed with my mind. It made me question so many things about myself. It made me feel so bad about myself. I know that it wasn't my fault. But you can't help but think that maybe you did something. What it did more than anything was make me know what some men are capable of. If you had seen Anthony's grandfather, he didn't look like a dirty old man. He looked like a harmless old grandfather. Yet I know he would have tried a whole lot worse if Anthony hadn't come back when he did.

That's why I talk to my daughter and my nieces. I tell them that they can tell me anything. And that if anyone—and I mean anyone—ever touches them or makes them feel funny, they better come and tell me. I tell them that they will be in more trouble if they don't tell.

I was at a family cookout a while back. You know those summer cookouts where the whole family gets together. There was music and card playing and a lot of laughing. I was there with my son, Tyran, and daughter, Egypt. It was at my sister's house in Jersey. Everyone was having such a great time until I lost my mind.

I had gone to the bathroom. And when I came out, I was looking for Egypt.

"Oh, she went for a walk with Micah," my sister told me. Micah was her husband.

"A walk?!" I said, starting to really lose it. "Where? Where is my child?!"

At this point I was on the verge of hysterics. We were in the kitchen, but even the people outside could hear me screaming.

"Calm down, Sandy," my sister said. "She's just with Micah, right outside."

"Where is she!" I screamed. "Where?!"

My sister was starting to get mad because in her mind was what I was really getting all upset about. Egypt was with her husband. So what was I trying to say? And, yes, that's exactly what I was saying. Not because Micah was a bad guy or I thought he would actually do anything to Egypt. I was acting out of my own experiences. This wasn't about my sister or my sister's husband or even Egypt. This was about me.

It didn't stop after Anthony's grandfather. Anthony's grandfather was just the beginning. One of my sister's boyfriends was at our house once a few years after that incident with Anthony's grandfather. You know my sisters are all much older than I am, and their boyfriends were basically grown men. We had a big house with lots of rooms and lots of places to hide, and I got caught in one of those rooms with one of my sisters' boyfriends. He got me a corner and forced me to touch him while he touched me inside my panties. I was about nine and started to scream. But once again, there was the threat.

"Shut up! Shut up!" he growled at me through clenched teeth.

"Don't you say nothing!" he said after it was over.

I eventually told Dawn. I was scared, but Dawn was my best friend and my protector. She got ahold of my father's gun and threatened him. Dawn was wild. She would often sneak my father's .45 out of its hiding place in the closet. She would scare me with that because I knew if anything really happened, she would use it.

"Oooh, you're taking daddy's gun?!" I said when I first saw her do it.

"Don't say nothing!"

"I'm not," I would say.

Dawn was so tough. She found out about this pimp who had been harassing me on my way to school when I was eleven. She had some words with him with my daddy's .45 and he left me alone.

And after Dawn had words with my sister's boyfriend, he never came back around, either. He must have said something to my sister because she confronted me and said I was lying about her boyfriend. She took his side, which was painful.

When you don't believe children, you rob them. I know what that did to me. I shut down. It made me not want to tell anyone because I didn't want to fight about it. From that experience I vowed I would never put any kid of mine, nor a niece or nephew, through that. If kids told me something happened to them, I would take their side no matter what.

Through all of these bad experiences, I still held out hope. I still had in my mind this fairy tale about love and being a princess and having a knight come and sweep me off my feet.

I used to read about these stories of love. I would see them on the soap operas that my grandmother used to watch and which had me hooked, too. All of these love stories. I would hear my little friends talk about their boyfriends and being in love and I wanted that. All I knew at this point were some dirty old men grabbing and poking me and making me feel weird and dirty.

So while that was all I knew, I also knew that there had to be more and I wanted to know what it was. I wanted somebody to love me. I wanted to have a boyfriend who would hold me and kiss me and tell me he loved me. I was seeking that.

And like the chameleon that I was, I wanted to fit in. All of my girlfriends were "doing it" and I wanted to be doing what they were doing. One guy who lived in my neighborhood was cool and popular. Everybody knew him and liked him. He was also cute.

I was thirteen and he was seventeen. And he told me he liked me. He started coming around my house and spending hours on my front porch talking. He was the first guy I really liked. He courted me for a couple of months. He was telling me all kinds of nice things that I wasn't used to hearing, such as how pretty I was. He said he wanted to make love to me, and that sounded so wonderful. I could imagine the romance and the gentleness. Making *love*. That had to be okay, right? I wanted him to be my first.

We did it in his basement and it was nothing like I'd expected. There was a lot of fumbling and rough touching, poking, prodding, and shoving, and then it was over just as quickly as it started. There were no tender kisses or warm caresses. I was expecting so much more. But what happened when it was over, I definitely didn't expect. In my mind he was my boyfriend now and he loved me. I told him that I loved him. And I asked him, "We're in love, right?"

And he said, "I loathe you."

I was so thrilled. I gave him a big hug and kiss, and he grabbed me and threw me off him.

"I didn't say I loved you, I said I *loathe* you!"

I had no idea what it meant, but I knew that it wasn't good and it definitely wasn't love. "What?!"

"Go look it up!" And he told me to leave.

When I got home, I looked up this word in the dictionary and it said, "To feel intense dislike or disgust for."

Wow. I had spent two or three months with this guy. He used to come around my house, walk me from school, talk with me for hours. This wasn't a onetime thing. He was really courting me. He was so cute, like the neighborhood prince. He was so charming, even my mom liked him.

I finally felt that I wanted him to be my first and he tells me he loathes me. It wasn't just the word, it was the actions. He didn't want to have anything to do with me after I had given him my virginity. I was crushed.

I found out from my friends it was all a setup. I was part of some bet that he had with his friends that he could get me to do it with him. It was cruel. I used to hear my girlfriends talk about their first time and how wonderful it was. Well, I didn't have any great memories.

You would think that those things would be enough for me to be more careful when it came to men. But I must have been really hardheaded because it seemed that all I attracted were the wrong kinds of men. Or maybe I didn't feel that I deserved better, deep down inside. Maybe I was attracting these "damaged" guys because I thought I could fix them. I don't know what my problem was. But I know now that the problem was me.

CHAPTER FOUR

Heaven or Hell

I WAS A FRESHMAN IN high school when I started going with Mike (not his real name). He was a sophomore and it was definitely an instant connection. He used to tell me all the time that he couldn't live without me and that he would rather die than see me with anyone else. That was so sweet to me at the time. I thought, *Wow, he must really love me!* And that's what I thought when he used to smack me up, too.

When I think about it now, I get so angry. But back then as this flat-chested, skinny girl who wanted so desperately to have a boyfriend, I didn't know any better. He was giving me attention and that's all I knew. I didn't know how wrong it was.

One time I wanted to go to a block party in our neighborhood. But Mike didn't want me to go because he couldn't go with me.

"You better not go!" he told me. "I better not hear that you went there."

Well, I really wanted to go. So me and one of my girlfriends went. I didn't stay long. But on my way home, we were walking down Merrick Boulevard, and there was Mike waiting for me.

"Didn't I tell you not to go!"

He grabbed me by my arm and I pulled away. Then he grabbed me by my hair and walked me down this side street. When I think about it, he knew what he was doing was wrong because he would always say, "Let's walk!" and take me to this out-of-the-way location before smacking me around. He didn't want anyone to see him doing it.

Mike was yanking me and I was struggling to pull away. He got me into the middle of this secluded block and smacked me in my face.

"Didn't I tell you not to go to that party!" He smacked me again.

"I just went for a few hours."

Whack! "Bitch, didn't I tell you!" He started cursing me out in between the smacking. Now this is a young guy out here like this and I was taking it. I finally got the nerve to break away, and before I could take off running, he grabbed me and sank his teeth into the side of my face. He bit me down to the white meat. I still have a scar on the side of my face to this day from that. I was in shock. My face was a mess, bloody and red from the smacking. When I got home, my mother asked me what had happened. And I lied. I told her that I gotten into a fight with some girls.

I didn't want my family knowing the truth because I knew

there would be real trouble. After that, I decided to leave him alone. But he wasn't going away. He kept coming around and begging me to be with him, telling me how much he loved me. Like a sucker, I went back to him. And of course he started back up with the craziness. We got into a fight in front of his house once. He was beating me and someone called the police. As they were pulling up, he tried to hit me and I ducked and his hand went through the glass of his front door. He was cut badly all the way up the forearm.

The cops were there, the ambulance showed up, and he was hysterical. They patched him up and had to put him in a strait-jacket because he wouldn't leave.

"I love her!" he was screaming at the top of his lungs. "I love her! I love her!"

I was so scared after that. I didn't want anything to do with him. When he got out of the hospital, he tried to come after me again. He cornered me one day in an alleyway on my way home from school. He started pulling and grabbing me, begging me to come back to him. I didn't want to and he started hitting me. Out of nowhere my sister Dawn showed up and she jumped on him like a wildcat. She started whipping his ass. And while she had him on the ground, I picked up this huge rock. I was going to bash his head in. I was so mad. A crowd had formed by now and one of the guys yelled out, "Don't do it, Sandy!"

I knew it would feel so good to do it. I would be rid of him forever. I wanted to just smash his skull in.

"Don't do it!"

I didn't do it, thank God. And even after all of that, I couldn't leave him alone. Once again, Dawn came to the rescue (this time by accident). As I told you, Dawn was wild and used to sneak out of the house and party and drink, and she was smoking. One time she was smoking in the basement in one of the converted rooms. She must have fallen asleep with the cigarette lit and she burned down the house. The basement and the first floor were completely ruined, and after the firefighters finished axing up and watering down everything, the house was unlivable. We were all homeless and we lost a lot of pictures and other things that could never be replaced.

A part of me was glad that the Anderson Road house had burned. Ever since I was little, I had, well, I don't quite know how to explain it. I had these gifts (still do). I see spirits and get premonitions and have visions. When I started living in the attic of Anderson Road, there was a huge walk-in closet. It started with me hearing whispers, voices in the closet. At first I was scared. I would get hysterical—so hysterical that my parents kept me home from school a couple of times. I was traumatized by it because no one else could hear the voices except me.

But I got used to it. And actually, I was comforted by them. I used to come home from school and spend hours in that closet, listening to the voices. I couldn't make out what they were saying, but there was some singing and humming and it was soothing. We later found out that a man had died in that house. So we called it the haunted house.

After our house burned down, my family had to split up and find places to stay while the house was renovated, which took like a year. My sister Patsy had some big-time job out in Utah, and she begged my mother and father to let me come live with her. She sold them on how good the school system was.

So I moved to Logan, Utah. Black population? Two—me and Patsy. Logan had one of everything—one gas station, one store, one bar (yes, those white girls had me drinking Coors Light), and one high school. You had to drive to the big city, Salt Lake, which was more than an hour away, if you wanted to see any black people. I was the only black at Logan High. Even the janitor was white. I grew up in Jamaica, where I don't remember seeing a white person, and moved to a predominantly black neighborhood in Queens. This was definitely a culture shock for me.

I knew going there what I was in for because Patsy warned me. But I was still nervous about it. So I hatched a plan. I was going to be like Richard Pryor in *Stir Crazy* ("Yeah, we bad!"). I was this tough New Yorker who wasn't going to take any shit. I wanted them to be scared of me so that they would leave me alone. I was loud and boisterous and off the hook. The toughest girl in school, Brigitte, had big, curly, bleached-blond hair. She used roll up a pack of Marlboros in her T-shirt sleeve. She said to me, "Sandy, you're tough!" If she was saying it, it had to be true. I was popular at Logan High. I was on the gymnastics team and everybody liked me. I didn't have any problems until the mayor's son and I got into it.

I was in the lunchroom being loud and telling my stories and everybody was crowded around. And the mayor's son said something like "Yeah, right, nigger!" Everyone stopped. Nobody had tested me before. But Jason, Mark, Peter, or whatever his name had decided he was going to be the one. He was the mayor's son and I guess he was feeling himself.

"What did you say?" I snapped. "Because if you said what I think you said, I'm going to smack the shit out of you!"

"Nigger!" he said again.

I went over and hauled off and smacked him as hard as I could. You could hear the smack echo through the whole lunchroom, and everyone was in shock. They called both of us to the principal's office.

They told me that I should have handled that situation better and that I should have told someone what had happened. But they made him apologize to me. I didn't have any problems after that. When I walked down the stairs, the kids would part like the Red Sea. After I smacked the shit out of the mayor's son, I really had the school on lock. I was in charge in school, but at home with Patsy was another story.

She was so strict with her rules. And of course I was breaking them all. I was drinking and smoking and hanging out, and she would give my mother detailed reports.

"So what!" my mother would say. "That's what teenagers do. They rebel. She'll be fine."

I loved my mother for that. But Patsy couldn't take me. As soon as the house was ready, she shipped me back to Queens. I was happy to be back home.

My father made sure that the closet with the voices was completely closed up. With the renovations, they must have closed up the ghosts, too. I was happy to see them go.

CHAPTER FIVE

Daddy's Girl

BY MY JUNIOR YEAR I was in full rebellion mode and it was driving my father crazy.

"You're such a dunce!" my father yelled at me. Those words hurt me more than if he had hauled off and hit me. I had brought home my report card and I had a few C's. I didn't see the problem. At least I didn't get any F's. But my dad thought if I could get a C, I could just as easily get an A if I worked harder. He was right. But I wasn't trying to work that hard. I was in high school and I was feeling myself.

I was going through this phase, becoming more and more popular. I had a little boyfriend and I was at a party every weekend. But to my father, I was throwing my life away and he had little hope that I would amount to anything.

I went from being his baby—the one who all of my siblings used to say was his favorite—to being a disappointment. I had his face. I was the one he took to Coney Island every summer. He used to take us all to the beach, but I was the one who would roll with him when he visited family. My father taught me how to ride a bike and how to drive.

I know he wanted the best for me. And calling me stupid and a dunce was his way of trying to motivate me. He knew I could do it.

I used to get good grades. I always had my hand up. I liked answering questions in class. I liked to learn, I liked being smart. But it also made me a target when I was in grammar school. I would raise my hand every time the teacher asked a question, and I could see a few of the kids roll their eyes. I didn't care, though—not until one of the kids told me that he was going to kick my butt at lunchtime.

I guess he had had enough of me showing everybody up and he was going to teach me a lesson. I remember watching the clock praying that lunchtime would never come. It felt as if I were waiting for my execution. When the clock struck twelve, my heart sank. I went to my teacher and told her that I didn't want to go out for lunch.

"What do you mean you don't want to go out?" she asked. "Everybody goes out for recess. You have to go."

So obedient me went out. No sooner had I landed on the playground than I was surrounded by a bunch of kids. The adults who watched the playground at lunchtime were nowhere to be found. These kids had formed a circle around me, and the boy who had said he was going to kick my butt was right there in my face. The next thing I knew someone pushed him into me, and it seemed as if the whole crowd of kids were attacking me at

But it didn't stop her. By the tir[...] he was getting ready and I was
was pretty much lost to him. So [...]m. He tied his tie and put on his
more from me. But calling me a [...]tle bit of cologne. I don't remem-

I imagined that cartoon with[...]ever forget the smell. I loved my
with the pointy hat with the w[...]ottle shaped like a car.
bold letters. That's what I was to [...]like any other. I didn't know that
home A's.   [...]uld see him alive.

I understood why I was a dis[...]t morning, my father said some-
couldn't see me as serious. One
[...]ar th[...] this suit and this cologne and I
[...]l my funeral."
[...]ni[...] that. "Daddy, please! You're not
[...]ou[...]ing to happen to you."
[...] Amazing Grace,' okay? And I want
[...]ty coffin."
[...]u[...]rk and I got ready to go to school.
[...]k told me to be home at a certain
[...]d to hang out with my best friend,
[...]g of being home early, the way my
[...]e[...]
[...] these boys. They had a car. I had
[...]ve to school. Sonya and I and our
[...]ith no idea where they were tak-

But I loved that man. We had [...]As the streets became unfamiliar, I
I used to watch him get ready to [...]en we crossed a bridge, I was like
child welfare department for the [...] in Far Rockaway, Queens. I told
protecting kids from abuse.   [...]o where they were taking us and

My father was sharp and had h[...]me. They refused to take us home
had to be just right. He had show[...]em. We weren't down with that.
knot when I was young, and fro[...]ut in the Rockaways. Anyone who
him with his tie.

knows Queens knows that the Rockaways are like in the middle of nowhere. Even the buses stop running after a certain hour. And by this time, it was after a certain hour. Sonya and I were stranded. Sonya and I had been through some shit together. This was minor, I was thinking, compared to some of the other craziness.

Sonya was seeing this guy. He was a thug type, a drug dealer who lived in the Forty Projects. She asked me to go with her to get some money because she wanted to go shopping. It was the weekend. I had the car. My father taught me how to drive, and being the youngest, there was always a car to drive at my house.

When we got to this guy's place, he was busy and told Sonya to come back later for the money. She said okay and asked him what time. He said to come back at seven thirty that evening. She said okay. I drove her back over to the projects, and when I pulled up to the front of the building, I got this knot in the pit of my stomach and a panic came over me. I got out of the car, and when I hit the front door of the building, I got this feeling— my inner spirit. The older I got, the stronger my gift would get. Sometimes it came as a feeling, other times I would get full visions. This time it was just a feeling, and that feeling told me something bad was about to happen.

As we started to walk up the stairs—because you know the elevator is never working in the projects—I couldn't breathe. I told Sonya, "Listen, we're not staying here long. And when you get in there, don't go lounging and sitting on the couch and getting comfortable, because we're leaving. And you need to stay by the door. Do *not* sit down! Stay by the door!"

I was so serious, she said okay.

"Just do that. Stay by the door, okay?"

"Okay."

When we got to the fourth floor, I put my hand to my throat, which was tightening up. Some shit was about to go down. We knocked on the door and waited while he took the ten locks off the door. *Click, click, click, click, click, click, click, click, click.* There was even a lock at the bottom of the door. *Click.*

By this point, my insides were beating loud like a drum. I went inside and stood right by the door. He locked the door back. *Click, click, click, click, click . . .*

Sonya went and sat down on the couch, just as I'd told her *not* to. Every five minutes or so, some dude would come into the apartment. That part wasn't so strange because there was always traffic in and out of this joint. It was part of the business. But I didn't move from the door. And as another guy came in, I stood to the side. Sonya's friend asked me to sit down and offered us something to drink.

"No, we're cool," I said, giving her the evil eye to get her ass up off the couch and come stand near the door with me while he went to get her some money. He got up and said, "Give me a few," as he left the room.

At another knock at the door, my insides jumped. I noticed guns on the table, and one of the guys who'd come in earlier picked up a gun. Sonya was still just sitting there as if everything were okay and it was not.

When that last knock came, my voice said, *Run!*

So when the last latch was taken off the door and it opened, I said to Sonya, "Sonya, run! *Run!!!!!*" and I pushed past whoever was at the door and hit the hall and the stairs, hoping Sonya was behind me. I didn't have time to look back for her, and I hoped like hell that she'd listened. Sure enough, she was on my heels. When I pushed past the guy at the door, I knocked him to the floor, which gave Sonya time to jump off that couch and hit the door, too.

She was right there as I jumped down stairs, taking four and five at a time. Thank God, people were on the stairs coming up, because guys were chasing us from the apartment, grabbing for us.

We got to the bottom, down all four stories, and hit the main door out onto the streets. My hands were shaking as I fumbled for my keys and hopped into the car. Sonya got into the passenger side and I sped off. I must have gone a hundred all the way to my house.

"I told you no sitting down!" I was screaming on Sonya when we got into the car and pulled off.

She was crying because it had sunk in what was going to happen. "Why would he try to do that?"

We found out from someone in the Forty Projects that a call had gone out that two prime chicks were in homeboy's apartment, ready for whatever. Their plan was to run a train on us, gang-rape us. They had the guns, they had stuff in the back to tie us up, they had everything. The apartment was filling up as we were there, and there were going to be many more. It would have been on and popping.

We joked later about how difficult a time they would have had trying to get at Sonya. She had really skinny legs and used to wear long johns under her pants to make her legs look thicker, so they would have had to pull through all of that. We had jokes, but it was far from funny. We had to laugh to keep from crying for real.

When I think about what would have happened if we hadn't run, if that voice hadn't told me to run, I would probably have been killed because I can't imagine just letting them run a train on me—all of those guys. *All of them?*

And it was weird because I didn't have a strange feeling earlier in the day. Everything was fine. The guy must have hatched that plan after we left. He knew when we were coming back, and so he called as many dudes as he knew. Sonya and I weren't project chicks. We were a little on the naive side. We weren't wild and slutty like that. We were stupid, though. And obviously that experience didn't stop us from getting in that car with a bunch of guys we didn't know. Once again, I knew we needed to get out of there.

We ended up stranded in the middle of nowhere and hitchhiking back to Rosedale.

This was in the days before cell phones and we couldn't call anyone to come get us. Besides, I was supposed to come straight home after school. There was no way I was going to call home and say that I was stranded in the Rockaways. We just had to get home the best way we could. Once we got to Rosedale, we ended up walking the rest of the way home.

It was beyond late by the time I got to my street. I had more than missed my curfew. I was prepared for an ass-whipping. But when I stepped into my house, I had another kind of weird, scared feeling in the pit of my stomach. I wasn't nervous about getting into trouble for coming home late, there was something else.

As soon as I walked in the house, my mom started breaking on me:

"You're out there running the streets . . ."

I noticed immediately that she was crying. My mother is not a crier. As I looked around the house, it was full. It was always full, but everyone was together, on the main floor, and they all had this sad look on their faces, and they, too, were crying.

"Pop-Pa is dead!" my mother screamed.

What?!

My sister Jean, who was crying, too, confirmed it. "Daddy's gone."

"What?! When? How?"

I had so many questions. I was a ball of confusion. I had just seen him that morning and he was fine. How could he be dead?

"At the hospital," Jean said. "Tonight."

My father suffered from diabetes and had some kind of attack after work and had to be rushed to the hospital. They said he put up a fight but he had died just an hour before I got home.

I bolted out of the house in hysterics. I was running, just running and crying. I blamed myself. If I were there, he wouldn't be dead, I told myself. I wasn't there for him. He knew something was going to happen to him. That's why he told me about "Amazing Grace" and his cologne and what he wanted to wear at his funeral. He must have known something. Why didn't I know?

I felt wrong. I felt worthless. I should have been there.

And what hurt the most was that everybody got to say good-bye to my father, except me. Even Dawn got to say good-bye. They told me he was asking for me, before he died. He was asking for me and I wasn't there!

I needed to make sure that he had everything the way he wanted in death—that was the least I could do. I told my sister Bev, who was making all of the arrangements, that daddy wanted to wear his favorite blue suit and that he wanted his cologne and "Amazing Grace" playing. She said she would take care of it.

When I got to the wake, I was a basket case. I couldn't stop crying and I could hardly stand. But I dragged myself to his coffin to make sure everything was the way he'd wanted. He had on his suit, but I couldn't smell his cologne.

"He wanted to wear his cologne!" I screamed. I had brought the bottle with me, just in case, and I put some on him. He was going to have it just the way he wanted it. The only thing he didn't get was his vision of all of us carrying his coffin. That couldn't happen. None of us were in any shape to carry our father's body to his grave. I could barely think straight, let alone carry my father's coffin.

I felt haunted during those days. Those feelings made it hard for me to connect to life. It wasn't that I wanted to die, I just felt disconnected from life—as if I were just kind of floating through. I was in the middle of a thin wall between this world and the next. I was a wreck. I had so many regrets. I had so many things I needed to do, that I wanted to say to him. That moment taught me that you never know. That you have to do everything you can with the people you love while they're here. And you have to listen to people, really hear them. My father was telling me something and I didn't want to hear him.

This lady, Miss Wanda, a friend of the family's who lived in Springfield Gardens, told me that I had a gift. She could see it. She had a gift, too, and she could see my torment. "Child, you have to let him go," she said. "You have to let your father go or else he won't get any rest."

She told me that my holding on made it impossible for him to pass over peacefully. The last thing I wanted was to stop my father from having peace. So as hard as it was for me, I did eventually let him go.

But I couldn't let go of what was inside me—my thoughts, my feelings about myself. My father left this earth thinking I was a disappointment. I didn't get a chance to show him what I could do, that I wasn't a dunce. I would never get to show him.

He wanted the best from us. I understood that. And I never worked as hard as I could have. After he died, I busted my butt so hard. It was my senior year and I got all A's and became the honor student he knew I could be. I wanted to prove myself to him—even after his death.

To this day, I have a problem with people if they call me stupid, even if they're playing with me. You know how people say, "You're so stupid!" when they think you're being funny or something. I still have issues because it strikes a nerve.

I believe part of the reason why I worked so hard to be something was to show my daddy that I could do it. When I gave my acceptance speech for the Grammy for best rap song, I spoke in my head to my father.

Look at me, Daddy. I made it. I finally made it.

CHAPTER SIX

Salt-N-Pepa's Here

I ENROLLED IN QUEENSBOROUGH COLLEGE because I was going to do what my father would have wanted—get a degree and be successful. I was taking care of school, but I was still very much a party girl. I spent my breaks in the cafeteria playing spades, snapping jokes, laughing, and being loud. As soon as I came through, everybody would shout out, "Hey, Sandy!" I was that popular.

Over in one corner by herself would be this girl with her head in a book. She was quiet and never hung out with anybody. Her name was Cheryl James. She would say hello when I would come over and speak, but that was it. I used to try to figure out what her problem was. We would invite her to play spades and she would say, "No, I'm okay."

41

Then one day Cheryl started circulating around the cafeteria, talking to people. She was trying to get people to fill out these applications to work at Sears. I later found out she was getting something like twenty cents for every application she brought in. I filled one out. I was looking for a job at the time and it sounded easy. All we had to do was convince people to get an extended warranty or a maintenance agreement on an appliance they bought from Sears. I had a gift for gab, so I figured this job would be no problem.

That next day I went down to Sears on Queens Boulevard and was hired on the spot. I started working the next day. I was put in this room with little cubicles that lined the wall. Each cubicle had a little desk, a phone, and a list. We were supposed to call the people on the list and get them to buy the extended warranty or service contract. Sears kept track of our sales on this board.

Cheryl's boyfriend, Hurby (Azor), was always at the top of the board. I was having a slow start. I was distracted. Too many people were in the room to entertain and have fun with. I was always joking around. Cheryl blamed me for her poor performance, too. She was saying that she couldn't stop laughing long enough to make her calls.

I think Hurby was using tricks to get people to sign up. He always had something up his sleeve. A lady would come around and make sure we were making calls. I couldn't stand her. She had a little notebook and would make marks in there noting us not doing our work. Of course, I would stop bugging out and pretend to be making phone calls when she came around. And as soon as she left, it was back to fun and games.

It was hard to concentrate on making those calls. And I hated people telling me no, which they did all the time. Cheryl was having a hard time, too, which she blamed on me, but I wasn't the only one distracting people. This guy named Martin worked there and would have us in stitches. He was trying to be a comedian and, boy, was he funny!

It was crazy when I look back on who was actually working for our little part of Sears at this time. There was me and Cheryl and Hurby. There were these two other guys, both named Chris—one was from the Bronx, the other from Queens. And there was Martin from Washington, D.C.—all working at Sears at the same time.

Martin was talking about how he was going to be famous, how he was going to be the next Richard Pryor. And he was always trying out his routines on us. Cheryl didn't think he was funny at all. I thought he was hilarious. He used to always tell us, "I'm going to be a star one day! You just wait and see."

He wasn't lying. Martin ended up in a couple of little movies with the two Chrises and then he blew up. He had his own TV show, then went on to be a superstar, making $20 million a movie. Today everyone knows him as Martin Lawrence.

The two Chrises ended up making it, too. Chris Martin, the one from Queens, and Hurby called themselves the Super Lovers and had a group together. Hurby later ended up managing Chris and the other Chris (Reid) in their group Kid N Play. But before all of this, we were just a bunch of kids working at Sears.

During that time I got to really know Cheryl and we became close. We were such opposites, though. She was so quiet, and I was, well, still am, the life of the party. I used to have to drag her to go out. Every now and then she would. I took her to a male revue once. We still laugh about that night. I remember it as if it were yesterday. I had on this cheetah outfit that was so short. I looked like Jane out of *Tarzan* with the ripped-up edges around this short dress. We got seats right on the front row.

This big, sexy, muscular dude comes out and starts to do his thing. He's taking it off and looks down and starts coming at me. He has the finger with that "Come here" thing going, and I was like "No, no, no!" He came over and grabbed me by both of my hands and started pulling me onstage. And I was looking at Cheryl and she was cracking up.

"No, no, no!" I screamed. "Cheryl, help me!"

Cheryl tried to pull me back, but this guy was strong and got me onstage. The next thing I knew he had me flipped upside down with my head in his crotch and my legs all in the air with his head between my legs. Now mind you, I have on the shortest dress in history and I'm trying to pull the thing up, but my panties and ass and everything are on display.

After he finishes his set, he puts me back in my seat and I was humiliated. Cheryl couldn't stop laughing. This made her night. I never went back to that club again. I was done.

Cheryl always got to have fun like that being around me because I was always getting into something—even when I wasn't trying. I was Lucy and she was Ethel, along for the ride. That's how our friendship started and that's how it's always been.

And because of my friendship with Cheryl, Hurby and I became friends, too. Hurby was in school studying music and art. He was really into music, and I have to admit that he definitely had an ear for it. But more than that, Hurby was driven. He had these ideas and wouldn't stop until he saw them happen.

I was working at Sears for maybe a month before he approached me about one of his ideas:

"I'm forming an all-girl rap group, and I want you to be a part of it."

A rapper? Me? Sure, I had been playing around with the Chrises because they were both trying to be rappers. Everybody tried some kind of freestyle back then.

My name's Sandy D in the place to be . . .

That was the time when MCs were hot. But I never saw myself as a rapper. I was just playing around. These little groups would always be on the corner spitting rhymes. And every summer there was a block party or party in the park with a deejay and an MC rocking the mic and some turntables plugged in the light posts. I used to go to the park jams and watch the MCs, but I was more interested in dancing and partying than I was in grabbing the mic. I enjoyed just being in the crowd.

Rappers were dudes. Even the few girls who were out there were either weak or hard. I couldn't see myself as either.

But the idea of being a part of a group sounded like fun. But . . .

"I don't know about this, Hurby," I told him.

"No one, I mean *no one* has an all-girl rap group like this," he said. "This will be hot! You can do this."

I decided to do it. I decided to go along with it, not thinking we would actually cut a record. And even if we did, what were the chances of it being a hit? Well, we were dealing with Hurby. I should have known.

He knew Marley Marl, who I think came from the same neighborhood in Flushing and Queensbridge. Marley Marl was *the* man back then. He was the house producer for the Juice Crew, which included Big Daddy Kane, Biz Markie, Roxanne Shanté, and MC Shan, who was his cousin. He also produced Eric B. and Rakim. He was one of the first to make sampling really big. Marley Marl had a radio show on WBLS with Mr. Magic. It was the first radio show dedicated to rap, and it was hot. If you were a new artist and you were played on Marley Marl's show, you had made it. Hurby had the connection and he had a plan.

One of the hottest songs out at this time was "The Show," by Doug E. Fresh and Slick Rick. Hurby had come up with a song that he called "The Showstopper," which was an answer to "The Show." It was dissing Doug E. Fresh and Slick Rick. Dissing and answer songs were really popular back then. Rap, back in the day, was all about messages and MC swagger. The MC battle—where a rapper would boast about something and another rapper would try to take him down or outdo him— was popular. One of the best songs during that time (next to ours, of course) was "Roxanne's Revenge," in which Roxanne Shanté responded to UTFO's "Roxanne, Roxanne." That song was huge, and Roxanne Shanté, who was only like fourteen, became a sensation. That gave Hurby ideas.

Hurby decided that an all-female rap group could work. And a dis song against the hottest group would work, too. This is when I started to get nervous. He wanted us to go up against Doug E. Fresh and Slick Rick! I listened to them on the radio. They were huge! And I wasn't a rapper.

"Do you know what you're doing?" I asked Hurby. "Are you sure about this. I don't know ..."

"Trust me," he said. "This is going to be a hit."

I was still nervous. I mean this was Doug E. Fresh and Slick Rick! We met after work at Hurby's house. He had a studio (a ghetto studio, no state-of-the-art equipment, just a mic and some turntables and a tape recorder) in his basement. He had given us the basic lyrics and the hook, and Cheryl and I added some of our own flavor.

Have you ever been to jams when people just stand?
And they pay to come in, and they don't even dance?

The song started off pretty nice. But then it got nasty with a bunch of lyrics dissing Slick Rick's fake gold teeth and his plastic Bally's and "booty Gucci shoes" and his funky cologne, and we dissed Doug E. Fresh for not being as smooth as he thought he was. When we were done, I thought it was good.

Hurby was happy. He took the tape (this was way before CDs and iPods) to his boy Marley Marl. That night Marley Marl played "The Showstopper," by this hot new group, Super Nature.

To tell you the truth I didn't get excited until I actually heard the song on the radio. That's when it sank in that I had recorded a record. Cheryl and I were together at the time, driving down Guy R. Brewer Boulevard when it came on. At first, I thought it was "The Show," but when I heard our voices on the first bar, I almost ran off the road.

We were riding in my hoopty. I always had a car, but this was a piece of shit. It was a Datsun 210 and was so rusted that the passenger side had a hole in the floor. The hole was so big that if I ran over a puddle, whoever was sitting in the passenger seat would have to lift his or her legs to keep from getting wet from the water splashing up.

But Cheryl wasn't worried about getting wet or her feet touching the ground when "The Showstopper" came on. I pulled over right there on Guy R. Brewer Boulevard and jumped out and was telling everyone on the street, "My song's on the radio! My song's on the radio!"

I had the volume turned way up, straining the cheap speakers in my car; I wanted everybody to hear it. I jumped on the hood of that Datsun (putting a couple more dents in it) and started rocking to the song. I was bugging. I was yelling and screaming and rapping right along with the song on the radio.

Cheryl just sat in the car. I think she was embarrassed. I didn't care. That was an amazing feeling, and I think from that day on, I was hooked. I wanted to keep that feeling going. Hurby was right. The song was a hit and was one of the most requested on Mr. Magic/Marley Marl's show. Soon the offers came pouring in for us to do appearances. Appearances? We hadn't even thought that far. We had just one song and no stage act.

So Hurby and Cheryl and I came up with a routine to go with the song, and we started booking parties and club dates. Hurby came up with a new look and a new name. He changed our name to Salt-N-Pepa, which came from a rhyme in "The Showstopper":

> *Right now I'm gonna show you how it's supposed to be*
> *Cuz we, the Salt and Pepa MCs*

Cheryl was light and I was brown. So that worked. I was kind of sassy and spicy like a pepper, and Cheryl was kind of laid-back and conservative and bland . . . like salt. We were opposites but we blended well, like salt and pepper. As far as our look, Hurby was on this Prince trip. At the time, Prince had these two girls, Wendy and Lisa, on either side when he performed. Hurby liked that. So he had us dressed like them. And I guess he was supposed to be Prince. (When we did photo shoots, it would be Hurby in the middle like Prince with Cheryl and me on either side, looking sexy.)

Our first appearance was at Inferno, this club in Manhattan. We had practiced this dance routine. People were just rapping. Hurby, again with his ideas, thought we needed to really do a stage show and dance. This was before the days of wireless microphones, so we had to work around the twenty-foot mic cords and get all of these steps down. Hurby went to Jamaica Avenue and found these paisley suits for me and Cheryl. Paisley? Yuck. Again, this was part of his Prince phase. And he had us in these high-high heels.

I was used to sneakers or my punk-rock boots and fishnet stockings. I hadn't mastered heels. But this was Hurby's vision, so I went with it. Backstage, Cheryl and I looked like two deer in headlights.

The only thing that took some of the pressure off us was Martin Lawrence. We had promised him that if we made it, he could open for us. Hurby made a deal that allowed him to do a set of his comedy before we performed. We could hear the crowd on the other side of the curtain laughing, so he must have been doing well. But when he was done, it was our turn. And I was scared.

They started our song and we came out and started our routine. The stage was made of wood, and there were spaces between each plank. One of my high-high heels got caught in between the wooden planks, and when I tried to do one of our steps, I got stuck. That wasn't bad enough, so Cheryl forgot her lines. It was a disaster. But the crowd didn't seem to notice. They were hopping and hollering and we got through it.

After the show, the club owner booked us for two more nights. So we did three shows in a row at Inferno, and each night was more packed than the night before. It was official: we were a hit.

It's funny, you hear all of these stories about rappers hustling around with their demo tape, begging somebody to listen to it and give them a deal. You hear about the rejection and how hard it was for them. Salt-N-Pepa never had one of those struggling stories. We got together. We made a song. It was a hit. We got a record deal. The album went platinum and the rest is history. It was almost too easy.

"Showstopper" was playing everywhere. Doug E. Fresh and Slick Rick never responded. I guess they knew that if they replied, that would make it an even bigger deal. Slick Rick did say in a magazine article, "We let them slide this time, but if they try that again, we're coming for them."

We would see them out years later and Cheryl and I were awkward with them at first. We would have our cheesy smiles in place and our nervous hellos. We didn't want any trouble. I'm glad we moved beyond that song because that whole dissing thing wasn't what we were about. We had a line in a song that said, "You're babbling like you're from Babylon," (or something like that, I don't quite remember). But people were saying that we were trying to dis LL. We didn't even know that Babylon was a place in Long Island at the time, and we definitely didn't know that LL lived there. But people were trying to start stuff. Thank God it got squashed.

Our rise was pretty quick and painless in the beginning. After "Showstopper" we were getting more and more requests to perform, which was good for Martin, too, because he got to open at a lot more places.

I knew we had really made it when we were booked to play The Fever in the Bronx—the birthplace of hip-hop. The Fever was the place featured in *Krush Groove*. This was the place where real rappers performed. The crowd there did not play. They didn't just give you love, you had to earn it. And if you were bad, they let you know. They were like the Apollo Theatre of the rap world.

I remember driving by there a few weeks before we were to perform. They had our name on the marquee: SALT-N-PEPA PERFORMING OCTOBER 24. When the date started narrowing down I was thinking, *Oh, shit!* We were actually going to perform at The Fever.

We worked on our routine every day. We had to come up with something special and it had to be perfect. We went to Jamaica Avenue and got new outfits. We picked out these white satin jackets and had SALT and PEPA stitched in black lettering on the back (SALT on the back of Cheryl's and PEPA on the back of mine). We didn't have a stylist back then, just Hurby and Jamaica Avenue.

I convinced Hurby to let us ditch those high-ass heels. I was back in my punk-rock flat boots, which worked even better with his Prince theme. Hurby came up with this new opening for us. Prince had a song called "Darling Nikki." We did a version of "Showstopper" over the "Darling Nikki" tune. But this version was way harder, way more nasty than the original— which played really well with The Fever crowd.

When the music started and the curtain went up, Cheryl and I were standing there back-to-back. It was dramatic. And the crowd went crazy.

I knew a guy named Ricky . . .

And we proceeded to talk about Slick Rick and Doug E. Fresh so bad that I'm embarrassed to even repeat any of it. I can't believe the stuff we were saying. We called them gay and everything under the sun. And the crowd said, "Ooh!" with every punch line. We had some nerve. Two girls dissing Mr. La-di-dah-dy. Slick Rick was the man. And Doug E. Fresh is still the man. He still rocks the party. When I see him today, it's nothing but love. He is always shouting us out and I really love what he does.

But back then for these girls from Queens to do what we were doing was unheard of. To come at them so hard and yet still be so sexy just made it happen. We rapped hard but looked sexy—that was our twist.

After we rocked The Fever, we started getting invited on major tours with Heavy D and the Boyz, Keith Sweat, LL, Guy. We were the only girls. These national tours meant we had to go on the road.

What was crazy was that we were still in school *and* working at Sears. Cheryl was the one that said, "Sandy, I think we have to drop out. We can't stay in school and tour like this." I knew she was right, but I couldn't imagine dropping out of school. That wasn't an option. I decided to take a leave of absence. I never officially dropped out. As far as I know, I'm still enrolled at Queensborough.

I told my mom what I was doing. All she said was "You better make sure you know what you're doing!"

I had no idea what I was doing. But I was going for it anyway.

CHAPTER SEVEN

My Scarface

WHILE MY CAREER WAS LOOKING up, my love life was also hitting some high notes. I had met this young, handsome, and rich—just my type—guy who was from around my way just before I got involved with Salt-N-Pepa. He was from the streets but he had some class. The tide had turned for me and I wasn't trying to holler at just anybody who came around. If a guy wanted to be with me, he had to work for it, and Tommy was willing to work for it. He pursued me hard and I was loving it.

Merrick Boulevard in Jamaica was similar to Flatbush Avenue in Brooklyn or Forty-second Street in Manhattan. It was the strip, the spot. And Tommy owned it all. He had a Laundromat, a sporting-goods store, a grocery store, a social club. He sponsored neighborhood basketball leagues and peewee football clubs. He was also a drug dealer.

I didn't find that out until much later. Maybe I always knew he was a drug dealer, but I didn't care enough at the time. I liked being around Tommy a lot and didn't want to think about anything that might mess up what we had. He was one of the first men ever to treat me nicely. He called me his princess. He was smart and funny and I liked his style. He was a little jealous (sometimes a lot jealous), though. But even that was attractive because it told me that he really cared about me.

With him I was living the rock-star lifestyle before I was really a rock star. Even when Salt-N-Pepa had that first album, I still wasn't making the kind of money that recording stars made. I was still living at home and still driving that Datsun. Tommy had a big house in a rich area of Long Island. He was the first person I ever knew who had a Rolls-Royce. He had several luxury cars, including a BMW and a Ferrari. He even had a yacht, which he kept in California. He was also the first person I knew to have a cell phone. Back then, cell phones were big and clunky and came in one color—ugly cream. Few people had cell phones because they cost so much. Tommy had several. He had one in his Rolls that popped out of the center console. And he had one that he carried around that he said was just for me.

"I only use this phone to call you," he told me. "This is your special, private line, and nobody else can call me on this."

Tommy was fly. He was flashy, but not the way a lot of dudes were flashy with all of the gold chains and that craziness. His stuff was tasteful. He did carry around a lot of money, though. Lots and lots of hundreds. For such a young man, he was also very mature. He had big dreams. I loved hearing him talk about his plans. He was going to take back the hood and turn it into a paradise. I was a part of those plans, he told me.

"Baby, I'm going to buy you your own island," he told me one night. "Do you know how many uncharted islands there are, just waiting for someone to claim them? One of them will have your name on it."

Sandy Island. I could see it.

I believed him. Tommy did everything he set out to do.

We were hanging hard together for almost a year. And it was great. Cheryl liked him, too. During this time she was going through it with Hurby. It seemed as though the more successful we became, the bigger Hurby's head got. I didn't think it was possible for him to get more full of himself, but he did. And he started doing whatever he wanted to do out in the open. He had all kinds of chicks on the side and was just rude and mean to Cheryl a lot in public.

It got so bad one summer that she ended up moving in with me. Yes, Cheryl stayed in the attic of my parents' house with me for an entire summer, and we didn't kill each other. It was kind of nice. I hadn't had a roommate since Dawn moved out. Unlike Dawn, though, Cheryl didn't like to party much.

I would be out almost every night and I would try to drag Cheryl with me. Every now and then she would come. Most nights she stayed in that attic watching TV or curling up with a book. I did hook her up with one of Tommy's boys, Tony. He was really cute and nice, too. We double-dated a few times. But Cheryl ended up going back to Hurby. It was tough because she couldn't avoid him. We worked together. He was the group leader, he was the manager, even though we had hired management. Hurby made all of the decisions. So he was always around. I felt bad for Cheryl, just as I know she felt bad for me when I was going through my bad relationships (and, boy, did I have a few of those).

But Tommy was one of the bright spots. I was with him almost every night. He would pick me up and we'd go out to eat at a nice restaurant—he exposed to me places I had never been to before, such as the Water Club on the East River and Carmine's, where you could get real Italian food. He exposed me to City Island in the Bronx, which put Red Lobster (one of my favorites) to shame.

It was all perfect—too perfect. Of course it couldn't last.

I got a call one night from Tommy, who had just gotten back from spending a few days in California on business.

"Baby, get ready because I'm coming to get you," he said.

He told me to throw some things in a bag and be ready when he came. He had a few stops to make first but would pick me up around eight. I was excited because Tommy always had some sort of surprise for me. As I was gathering my things, my inner spirit clicked in.

Don't go with him!

This voice came out of nowhere. My first reaction was to ignore it.

Don't go! Don't go!

Some people call it intuition, but to me it was just God or a spirit from God telling me not to go. I have been blessed with a gift since I was little. And as I've gotten older, the gift has gotten stronger. It started when I was about five or six, when my imaginary friend was Jesus. Yeah, I know it sounds crazy, but that's who I thought my imaginary friend was, and I believe He has been looking over me ever since.

Anytime I ignored that voice, I would regret it. I knew I couldn't go with Tommy on this night.

A few minutes later, Tommy called me to see if I was ready.

"Um, no," I told him, stumbling over my words. "I'm really tired. I think I'm going to stay in tonight."

He was quiet for a minute on the other end. I thought I was going to pass out. I couldn't breathe. I was nervous, hoping he didn't know I was lying.

"What's wrong with you?" He could sense something was up.

"Nothing. I'm just tired. I'm not feeling well. I think I'm going to just go to bed."

There was no way I could tell him that a voice was telling me to stay away from him. As soon as we hung up, I grabbed my Bible. I remember crying and hugging my Bible.

"Please, please, please, God!" I was hysterical at this point.

I didn't know what was going to happen. But I knew *something* was going to happen. And I wasn't supposed to be with Tommy when it did.

I sat there praying. I prayed so hard, I fell asleep holding my Bible. The phone woke me up. It was my friend Cyan.

"Girl, turn on the TV!" she screamed, not even saying hello. "Tommy's on TV."

I turned on the news and there was Tommy, with a blue hoodie over his head, being led away in handcuffs. A whole SWAT team was at his house. Had I been there that night, I would have been arrested, too. Everyone with Tommy, everyone in his house, was arrested. And every single one of them did time. They tried to subpoena me, but I didn't know anything. Tommy purposely never talked about his business around me and I purposely never asked.

The authorities were really trying to get me, though. They were showing me pictures of all of Tommy's stuff. They showed me the yacht.

"Have you ever seen this?" they asked me.

I had never been on it. Then they showed me pictures of me and him in the Rolls-Royce. It was crazy. They must have been following him for months, staking him out. It was really funny seeing myself in those blurry pictures. And I was thanking God that I was never involved in any way. But I was still nervous. His trial was crazy, and when they handed down the sentence, I couldn't believe it.

Tommy didn't get a plea bargain, no break, nothing. He was convicted of tax evasion and money laundering and conspiracy to sell drugs. He was sentenced to thirty-five years in federal prison. No chance for parole. He was only twenty-five. He's still in prison today.

He had everything. And in one flash, it was all taken away—including his freedom. His millions—and they said they found about $3 million, but they knew it was more—went to his lawyers.

Through this whole ordeal, Tommy wanted to see me. My family, especially my sister Dawn, were telling me to stay away from him. It was best. I was on the verge of becoming a star, a real star, and I didn't need the baggage of that kind of drama, even if I really liked Tommy. And I did. Besides, Salt-N-Pepa were getting booked to do major tours, which meant we had to practice our routines and then we would be on the road almost nonstop for months. There was no time to visit Tommy.

I must have made an impression on him or maybe it hurt him that much that I never went to see him, because years later people from around our way who knew Tommy would tell me, "Tommy's looking for you." He still wanted me to visit him in prison.

I couldn't bring myself to do it. I didn't want to see him like that. At the same time, I was glad that I didn't get so involved with him the way I could have.

His previous girlfriend got arrested and had to serve about five years. She must have known something. She was with him when he was coming up in the game. I was glad that I was spared. That could have ruined all my plans before I even got started.

CHAPTER EIGHT

Big Fun

FOR ME, ONE OF THE wildest things in the beginning about being a part of Salt-N-Pepa was getting to meet some of the pioneers and the major stars of hip-hop. I was just as much of a fan as I was a performer. I didn't really know or understand how much Cheryl and I were doing at the time to pave the way for other females in rap and hip-hop. We were just doing our thing. And Hurby made the process so miserable—especially for Cheryl—that we didn't really have time to think about how other people were seeing us. I knew we had fans and they loved us. But for me, I wasn't thinking that we would ever have the kind of impact that Run-D.M.C. and LL and Doug E. Fresh and Grandmaster Flash and KRS-One and Public Enemy and all of those other acts and groups were having. I couldn't see us in the same category as those guys back then. I do today, though.

Early in the game, we had that one song that was a hit. We didn't have a string . . . yet. And I remember being honored to be invited to one of our first industry events, a party for *Krush Groove,* which was the hottest rap movie out. This movie starred Blair Underwood and a bunch of rap stars such as Kurtis Blow, Run-D.M.C., the Beastie Boys, the Fat Boys, LL. It was based on the rise of Russell Simmons. I knew about Russell Simmons, but I didn't know then that Run was his brother or how much he was connected to the beginning of hip-hop.

All of them were at this party, and I was sick as a dog. But I wasn't going to miss it, either. My eyes were big as I saw one star after another. I was there to represent Salt-N-Pepa. This was like our coming-out party where we were supposed to establish our place in the game among these stars. But I was too busy stargazing.

When I saw LL Cool J, I almost passed out. What a cutie. I had such a crush on him. (Who didn't?) Years later, we ended up on tour together and became friends. We hung out a little bit and he even came to my house once, which bugged me out. But he would never go *there* with me. He was such a tease. I wasn't one to throw myself at anyone, and I guess he was getting that all of the time—women throwing themselves at him. I didn't and he never ever tried anything. He was respectful—damn him! When *Krush Groove* came out, he wasn't a star yet. But he was still cute.

While I was standing there trying to make goo-goo eyes at LL, this big guy came over and said hello. I recognized him as one of the Fat Boys, Prince Markie D. They were really big back then (yes, both ways). They had a couple of gold hits, including "Fat Boys," and "Stick 'Em" and "Can You Feel It." Prince Markie D was the cutest. I wasn't into fat dudes and had never dated anyone overweight. But Markie had this swagger about him that was sexy. He was so confident.

"You okay, sweetheart?" Markie said, looking concerned. I thought I was putting on a good face, but apparently my sickness was coming through.

"No, I have a very bad cold," I told him through my sniffles.

"Ooh, stay away from me," he said jokingly. But he stood there and talked with me for a few minutes. A lot of people were in the room, and Cheryl and Hurby were somewhere mingling. Markie left, then came back about fifteen minutes later with some cold medicine. He had sent someone out, a driver or someone, to get me some cold medicine. He was that concerned.

That was one of the nicest things a guy had ever done for me. I was impressed. I thanked him and he went on about his business. I took the medicine and didn't think anything else about it, except that Markie D was a nice guy.

The next day, he called me. I don't know where he got my number. Back then people just gave out your number. There was no protecting anyone's privacy.

"I'm calling to see how you're doing," he said.

Wow. He scored another point. I thanked him again.

"Well, when you're feeling better, I'd love to take you out."

I was excited. I mean he was a real celebrity. And he was asking *me* out. I couldn't wait to tell Cheryl. She was less than encouraging at first.

"Well, he's really big!" she said.

She started teasing me because she was saying that he was fat *and* he was a big shot and was asking me if I could handle all of that. But she eventually came around. After Tommy, it was time for me to get back into the swing of things. I was ready. And Markie D would be a nice change of pace—an industry guy. That would be different. Actually, the whole thing would be different. Could I handle all of that? I didn't know. He had to weigh about three hundred pounds. I was thinking, "Why didn't LL ask me out?"

I was a little nervous about dating Markie because I didn't want to hurt his feelings and what if I wasn't attracted to him in that way? But all of that went away once I spent some time with him. He was so confident, so solid, so strong in himself, that you couldn't help but feel the same way about him. Heck, he not only was okay with being fat, he made fat fashionable. He made it okay for everyone else, too. Just think about the acts that came out around the time of the Fat Boys, such as Heavy D and the Boyz, Chubb Rock. Being big was definitely not a bad thing in rap.

Being fat is what made Markie a star. So if it didn't bother him, it didn't bother me. I used to play with his belly and pretend that I was making a pizza on that sucker.

We dated a few times before things got serious. We were a couple pretty quickly. He invited me to his house out in Rosedale. I had been to nice neighborhoods and stayed in fancy houses hanging with Tommy. But Markie's house was really nice, too. I knew he was successful, but I didn't know you could make that kind of money rapping. There was no *MTV Cribs* back then. Cheryl and I were making about $200 a night performing, and we hadn't seen any real money from our record deal yet. But seeing the way Markie was living showed me that you could get rich rapping.

What freaked me out was that I'd lived in Queens most of my life and had never seen the part of Queens that he lived in.

The section was tucked near the Green Acres Mall, which I had been to many times. But I had no clue about these beautiful homes and the wealth around them.

I used to go out to stay with him on the weekends. The weekends turned into three times a week. And that turned into every day. I ended up moving in with him after just a couple of months of dating.

In the beginning it was great (isn't it always?). When I was on the road, he would be jealous. And when he was on the road, I would be sitting in his big house by myself thinking the worst. I had seen how the groupies were. I saw the kinds of women that would be flocking to these rappers, and Markie was a sex symbol, believe it. But his jealousy was way worse than mine. He was unreasonable.

It started with him limiting my friends.

"I don't like that Sonya girl," he would say. "I don't want her coming around here."

Then it would be that he didn't want me hanging out with her at all. One by one he would tell me that he didn't want me hanging with this one or that one. He didn't want me hanging with my own sisters. And I, the dummy, was listening to him. I wanted to make him happy. He wanted to know where I was every second of the day and whom I was hanging with. At first, I thought it was cute. I liked how strong he was with his demands, too. Looking back, I know I attracted these controlling men because I missed my daddy. I missed having him in my life, and I needed to have a man to take care of me and whom I had to answer to.

I also realized that by my being so obedient it attracted the kind of guy that would be abusive. Markie wasn't physically abusive, but he used to yell and argue a lot, and he did that crazy stuff such as try to cut me off from my friends and family.

If I told him I was going to the store, when I came back, he would ask for the receipt to prove that I went. And I would actually give it to him instead of saying, "F you!" I couldn't take it. Finally, I packed up my stuff and left.

But I had a hard time being alone. I wanted to have a man. I didn't want to be out there dating. I liked being in a rela-tionship—even a bad one. At the same time, Cheryl was going through her drama with Hurby. So we had each other's shoulder to cry on.

We would be onstage working it, playing to the fans, enjoy-ing their feedback. Off the stage, we were both a mess—she with Hurby and me with whoever it was at the time.

CHAPTER NINE

Give Props to Hip-Hop

EVERYTHING HURBY SAID WOULD HAPPEN was happening. I have to give him credit. He wrote most every song. Came up with our image (we added our own flavor, of course). He hustled to get our records played. He had all of the connections. We were all making more money than I ever imagined—it was more than working at Sears, that's for sure. And I had found something that I was really good at and that I enjoyed doing. I was pretty happy.

After "Showstopper," we recorded "Tramp." This was an edgy song that I absolutely loved. Back then, if you cut a record, there would be an A side—which was supposed to be the hit, the one that you did the video for—and a B side. "Tramp" was on the A side of the single. On the B side Hurby had us do this song called "Push It." I hated it. Even Cheryl didn't like it. It was too pop. With "Showstopper" being so big, there was a lot of talk about us being crossover artists. For a rapper in those days, being crossover was not a compliment; it wasn't a good thing. We didn't want to be considered crossover or pop because we were trying to be taken seriously as rappers, especially being girls. So hearing "Push It," I was like "Hell no! This is corny!"

But Hurby said, "You're going to record this!" So we did.

We went to Gordy's studio in Brooklyn and did it. Gordy was a producer and came up with the beat. And we recorded it in his makeshift studio, which was a step up from Hurby's.

We did the video for "Tramp," which Hurby came up with this whole movielike scenario for. Chris (Play) was in the video playing a tramp, of course. There were guys playing horns in it. Cheryl and I were going through these different scenarios where different guys were showing themselves to be tramps. We had these cute white shorts on for the dance scenes of the video, and I thought the whole concept was hot. Videos weren't that big a deal then. There weren't any twenty-four-hour video shows on. Fab Five Freddy was one of the first with a rap show on MTV. There were only a few places you could see your video. Not like today.

We were proud of our little video for "Tramp" because it was our first. We just knew that song was going to be a hit, too. But when the record came out, what was blowing up on the radio and in the clubs was "Push It." They played it so much that before we knew it that song was a bigger hit than "Showstopper." We had to rush to do a video for it. We decided to tape one of our concerts and turn it into a dance video with the crowd and everything. What was cool was that we didn't have to prompt the crowd to scream. They were totally into the song on their own. And that video turned out to be great.

In between the "Tramp" and the "Push It" videos Hurby made some changes to the group. Initially, Salt-N-Pepa had a female deejay named Spinderella. Her name was LaToya and she was from the neighborhood. She was okay on the turntables, which was good enough for the look Hurby was going for with his all-female group. But LaToya wasn't really into it. She didn't show up to the practices and missed a few appearances. Even though "Showstopper" was a hit, I guess she didn't see Salt-N-Pepa really going anywhere. Besides, she was in love. So she left the group to be with her man.

"Okay, girls, we're going to try something new!" Hurby announced as he started bringing new girls around to audition for Spinderella.

Hurby auditioned a bunch of girls, including Wendy Williams (New York City radio talk-show host and self-proclaimed Queen of All Media). Hurby was going for a look; he didn't care whether the girl could really deejay, he figured that he could teach her how to spin records.

One day he showed up to rehearsal with Dee Dee (Roper). She was young and pretty—which was a must for Hurby. And she had some deejaying skills already. She wasn't DJ Jazzy Joyce or anything, but she could do the basics and was eager to learn more. Her being pretty was Hurby's first concern. Cheryl's eyebrows raised when Dee Dee came into the group, and they didn't quite hit it off. I already knew the deal, but I kept my mouth closed, or else.

I immediately hit it off with Dee Dee. She was a great fit for me. We both liked the same foods—supreme nachos and Red Lobster. We would both get a craving on the road and head to Red Lobster together. She liked to talk, I liked to talk. She liked to party, I liked to party.

The other Spin was quiet and kept to herself, and she and Cheryl were pretty much on the same wavelength. But Dee Dee became my hang-out partner. On the road she would go with me to the after parties or to the clubs or hang out in the hotel's lounge or lobby. Cheryl would never hang out when we were on the road. She would always be up in her room watching television or sleeping. But Dee Dee was good to go. Cheryl was being loyal to Hurby. But I would often see Hurby at the after-party or in the hotel lobby or bar, too. Of course, I couldn't say anything. He was always with the threats: "You can be replaced!" He pretty much told me that I needed to just be happy to be a part of this. And I was. So I had to zip it.

I was still learning a lot about the business and myself. In the beginning, I know I drove Hurby as crazy as he drove me. I was rough around the edges, and he wanted us to be refined and classy. I loved to hang out and party, and he wanted us girls to keep to ourselves. I was a free spirit and he was a control freak. Cheryl was obedient to Hurby, so for her the whole experience was just work. But I was determined that I was going to enjoy it.

We got our first big check from signing our record deal with Next Plateau Records. I did a very ghetto thing with a chunk of it and went to Jamaica Avenue and bought a bunch of jewelry. I got some gold fronts and had them put my initial on one tooth and some diamonds on another. I was one of the first to have diamonds in my gold fronts—yes, before the Cash Money Millionaires and Flava Flav and all of those boys, Pepa was rocking gold fronts with diamonds. I also bought this nugget ring that cost me about $700 on the avenue, where everything was discounted. That's a lot of money even today. I loved that ring.

I remember one of our first performances at a major venue was at the Nassau Coliseum. I was so excited. It was sinking in that this music thing was going to take us places. We had on our new outfits and I was wearing my new nugget ring. The place was packed and the crowd was screaming for us. The lights were low and we had our dancers and Hurby and everyone on the stage. We were performing "Push It," and I was waving my hands in the air, getting into it. It was a high-energy song with lots of moves, and the next thing I knew, my ring flew off into the crowd.

"Hold up! Hold up!" I screamed, right in the middle of the performance. "Turn the lights up! Turn the lights up!"

Cheryl was trying to continue as if nothing were going on. She was totally ignoring me. But I wouldn't stop.

"Hold up, I said! My ring is in this crowd somewhere!"

When it was obvious that I wasn't going to continue until they turned up the lights and started looking for my ring, they turned the lights up. I jumped down into the crowd and started breaking on people, warning them that they had better not have stolen my ring. I was ready to fight. Poor Cheryl was trying to play it off.

"Oh, it's a very special ring," she was telling the crowd. "Her grandmother gave it to her and it has special value."

"Is this it?!" a girl shouted, holding up my ring. Yep. I was so happy. I got my ring back and went back onstage and attempted to pick up where we had left off. Cheryl joked that the crowd wasn't quite feeling us the same way after that display by me. Yes, I know it was ghetto. But that's how I was back then and I didn't care. Hurby threatened to replace me after that, but he didn't. When you're successful, you can overlook some things.

And Salt-N-Pepa was officially successful. After "Tramp" and "Push It," our first album, *Hot, Cool & Vicious,* sold more than a million copies. It was the first rap album by a female group to do that. Actually, it was one of the first rap albums *period* to sell more than a million copies. Only Run-D.M.C. was selling like that. Today an album is number one for like a week or two. Back then, if you had a hit album, it was a hit for a while. *Hot, Cool & Vicious* stayed at the top of the charts for almost two years with a string of hits such as "My Mic Sounds Nice" and "I'll Take Your Man," but "Push It" was the biggest hit. That song made it all the way to Europe.

Cheryl didn't really like that song. Years later when we came back together, that was one of the songs she didn't want to perform again. Why? Because too many people thought we were saying, "Ah, pussy. Pussy good!" I would say to her, "Cheryl, *you* know we're saying *push it*! Why do you care what people think?" But she hated that, especially when we went down South. They just knew we were talking about pussy down South. I thought it was hilarious. But for Cheryl, she didn't want to be associated with that.

Push it, pussy, who cared, it was a hit! And Salt-N-Pepa were laying down something that no female rap group had done before, and no female rap group have done since. We were selling records like the men.

And it was happening like a fairy tale—easy. I didn't do anything special to have all of these things happen so quickly. It was as if we had the Midas touch. Everything we did seemed to be a hit. The only thing that could stop us was us.

Of course, there was another side to this business. There was definitely a dark side, a grimy side. It was a business, after all. While touring around the country doing shows, you needed to have a road manager—somebody who made sure the dates you booked checked out and who made sure you got paid. Hurby was actually part of the group, so he couldn't worry about the stage show and handle the business. So he hired these guys to manage us.

I don't know where he found these guys, but they seemed like straight-up pimps. T (not his real name) and Ned were with us for about a year when Hurby decided that we needed to move in another direction. Cheryl and I were making like $500 apiece per show, and I have no idea what Hurby was getting. But I was happy with my money. But Hurby felt that T and Ned were taking more than their share and fired them.

Well, T was mad as hell when he found out and decided that he wasn't having it. He decided to put together a Salt-N-Pepa group of his own and tour them and get paid. We showed up to an appearance one evening and the guy at the door told us that Salt-N-Pepa had already arrived and wouldn't let us in.

Again, this was before MTV and all of that. This was before rappers were superstars, except for Run-D.M.C. and the Beastie Boys, who were basically rock stars. We had huge hits, but were still not really superstars. Nobody was stopping us on the street for our autographs back then. So people knew the name of the group, but as far as this guy at the door was concerned, Salt-N-Pepa were already in there performing.

"What?!" Hurby said. "*This* is Salt-N-Pepa!"

Hurby was about to lose his mind and was standing there arguing with the guy at the door, but it wasn't working. They still wouldn't let us in. Hurby found a way to sneak in through a side door and sure enough, two girls were onstage lip-synching our "Showstopper" and "Tramp," doing some wack dance moves. T and Ned figured they could just replace us and make all of the money themselves. They were hustlers for sure, and I swear that T was a pimp.

When the show was over, Hurby, Cheryl, and I were waiting for T and Ned.

"I want my money!" Hurby shouted at them. "If I don't get my money, I'm calling the cops."

Why did he say that? T and Ned were real thugs, and they rolled with this huge guy who looked as if he just got out of prison and they sicced him on Hurby. He started chasing Hurby down the street.

Cheryl and I were left there now arguing with T and Ned about our money and replacing us. Ned was really cool, just kind of listening and not doing much, but T was getting really mad. Cheryl, with her little self, was never afraid to get in some-body's face. In fact, she never backed down from an argument, it didn't matter how big a person was. So she was all up in T's face screaming, and all of a sudden he just hauled off and punched her right in the face and knocked her straight out. T then picked her up and punched her again. I jumped on his back and tried to poke his eyes out. I was going crazy on him.

I never saw anything like it. I was scared but I couldn't just stand there and do nothing or run like Hurby. So I started fight-ing. T swung me off him and grabbed me, and I just knew he was about to punch me out, too. I could see it in his eyes. But something stopped him. He just dropped me and walked away. Hurby was still running around somewhere trying to get away from prison dude.

I went to a pay phone across the street and called my family, and it seemed that in minutes my cousins and some of my sisters were there. I was crying and Cheryl was just coming to. We got her up and took her to a hospital. She needed stitches in the back of her head. It was a mess.

I realized from that day that we were in business and we had to get more serious about our business. We needed to know whom we were dealing with and what people were doing with us and our money. Cheryl's mom was good with money, and she managed our books for a while. I had a lot of smart sisters, but nobody knew anything about the music business. This was a different beast. But it was getting serious.

All I knew was that I was part of a group, Salt-N-Pepa. But I wanted to be more involved in things, and I started asking questions. That's when things began to go really wrong between Hurby and me.

CHAPTER TEN

Hurby Hate Bug

I WAS ALWAYS CAUGHT IN the middle between Hurby and Cheryl, or I was always the odd one out. Hurby and Cheryl were boyfriend and girlfriend when I met them. The group was Hurby's idea. Cheryl wrote a lot of the lyrics; she was the lead rapper in the group. And while they both used to remind me from time to time that I could be replaced, I never believed that. I never believed that there could be a Salt-N-Pepa without me. Sure, we replaced Spinderella a few times before finding Dee Dee (Roper). But I don't believe that there would have been a Salt-N-Pepa without me.

But when I got in Hurby's face about a decision I didn't like or when I threatened to tell Cheryl about his cheating, he would threaten me.

"We can find a new Pepa anytime," he would say. "Keep talking and I will find another Pepa."

I didn't think it would work with anyone else but me, but I didn't put it past Hurby to try. And that was the thing about him. He could be so nasty that I never wanted to push him to that point because I loved being a part of this group. I loved being Pepa. So I had to walk a tightrope.

I started getting wise to the things that Hurby was doing with the business. He was now playing the part of T and Ned, our first managers, who tried to replace us and steal our money. Hurby was controlling everything and giving us whatever he thought was appropriate. I had no idea how much money we should be getting until I started asking questions.

The question-asking wasn't about me. I never saw myself as an individual. To me Salt-N-Pepa was Cheryl and me. And the things that I did and wanted to do were about *us* getting ahead and *us* getting what we deserved.

Initially, I did take a backseat. I did feel just grateful to be there. And Hurby had a lot of control and power, some of it because he was Cheryl's boyfriend. She often had to choose between doing what was right for her relationship and doing what was right for the group. A lot of times the group took a backseat. So I had to step up. I took my place as part of this group and made some moves.

I credit Louis Burrell for giving me the ammunition I needed. Louis was the brother and manager of MC Hammer. We were on tour with Hammer. He had *Let's Get It Started,* which had the hit "Turn This Mutha Out," and we were still riding *Hot, Cool & Vicious* with "Push It." Hammer was big, but he blew up with the next album, *Please Hammer, Don't Hurt 'Em.* After that he had cartoons, a hundred-plus entourage, and the whole nine.

He had a pretty big stage show when we were out with him, but nothing like what he eventually got.

We were the headliners for this tour, which also featured Will Smith. He was calling himself the Fresh Prince, and he and DJ Jazzy Jeff had a hit song out, "Parents Just Don't Understand."

I thought Will was really cute and we would hang out a lot on the road. He liked to take care of me and never let me spend a dime. He was that kind of guy, real generous. I remember when they won their first award, he asked me to go out with him afterward. He was so excited. We were walking along the street getting ready to grab something to eat, and he just gave this homeless guy a $100 bill.

I sometimes kick myself when I think about what could have been. He was so nice to me, but I really wasn't feeling him. I guess I couldn't appreciate a nice guy like Will Smith. He wasn't thug enough. I was attracted to thugs and hoodlums, the jerks and mean guys. Will was too nice for me.

I liked people like Louis Burrell. He was rough, he was street, and he didn't pull any punches. He would walk around with a cane and a pimp hat. He always referred to women as "bitches." Even with all of that, I liked him.

One night Louis and I were hanging out and the talk got around to business. Louis was all about the business. He asked me about our deal. And I told him what little I knew. We were selling millions of records, and Cheryl and I were splitting six points. I didn't understand the whole point system and didn't know whether that was good or bad. But I soon found out.

"You dumb bitch!" he said. "Let me tell you something . . ."

And Louis began to break it down. He started telling me what we were supposed to be getting, and with the numbers we were selling that we should even be getting bonuses.

"I was told only Michael Jackson gets that kind of deal," I told him.

I knew we weren't anywhere near as big as Michael Jackson.

"I don't give a shit what they *told* you!" he said. "This is what you can get, and this is what you should be getting."

It was crazy. He was so raw with what he was telling me, and I felt dumb for not knowing more.

Hurby was everything. He was the manager, the producer, he was part of the group. How could he have had our best interests at heart with his hands in so many pots! He couldn't have our best interests at heart with his hands in so many pots. He hired our managers. Whom would they be loyal to? He hired the accountant, and the lawyer, too. No one in my family knew anything about the record business. Neither did anyone in Cheryl's. Her mom tried to keep the books. But this thing was big. We had to rely on Hurby.

I'm not mad at Carol, our manager, and her team. They did make us more famous and bring us more opportunities. But how much did we give up for that? Did they take more than they should have? I knew we needed someone to check them. And having Louis in my corner was just the ticket.

I went to Cheryl first to try to convince her to do something. But she wouldn't go against Hurby. When I came back with Louis, she told me to go ahead and do it.

It was hard for me because I knew Cheryl wanted to leave Hurby. I knew she wanted to walk away, but I also knew that she was scared. She felt that we needed Hurby, that we couldn't do it without him. But that wasn't true. We could get other producers. We wrote our own lyrics and choreographed our own shows by this time. Cheryl was really into shaping our look. We *could* do it without him.

But I could see Cheryl would not be down with getting rid of Hurby—at least not at this point. So I figured the least she could do was to work hard for us to get a bigger piece of the pie, for us to get what we deserved in terms of points.

Louis told me I could renegotiate our deal. Actually he said, "Bitch, you better go get your money!"

Salt-N-Pepa was selling millions of records. But Cheryl and Sandy were making peanuts. You remember the stories of TLC and how they were selling so many albums and they were all broke, and people were wondering how that could be. Well, I know how that could be because Cheryl and I were living that before we renegotiated.

Our tour money had gotten a lot better. But the money we were making from the album wasn't much more than what I would have got had I become a psychologist. We're selling millions but weren't bringing home anything close to millions.

And what was crazy about it was that I was the only one fighting for us to get more—to get what we deserved. Cheryl and I were fighting each other. She didn't want to rock the boat. And I'm like "Fuck that! I will sink this boat if we don't get what we ask for!"

After Louis broke down the math, it was on. He made me set up the meeting with Hurby and Carol. And I did. He told me what to say, and they knew that I was talking to Louis.

It always seemed like Carol and Hurby used to try to keep Cheryl and me away from people. They would never leave us alone. Anytime anyone came around, there was Carol right there. I believe they especially worked on Cheryl. Not only did they have the industry thinking we were these stuck-up girls, they were working on Cheryl to make sure that she would side with them against me. Divide and conquer.

When Cheryl went on vacation, Carol would be right there with her getting a tan. How often does management travel with an artist? They never traveled with me. Not once. So when it came time to make a decision, if Cheryl sided with them and I didn't, I would be lost. That's where the resentment came in from me. Cheryl was naive, so naive. And it strained our relationship. She couldn't see it. I saw it. I came off looking like the crazy, jealous friend. Of course, I did get jealous of the situation I was in. These people were able to do their thing and I couldn't do anything about it. And I had to keep quiet and bottle it all up or lose all that I worked for. You would be resentful and jealous, too.

So I was grateful for Louis Burrell. And Suge Knight, who was also talking to me about coming over to Death Row. He, like Louis, didn't give a fuck! And Carol and Hurby were scared of him, too. I decided not to go with Suge, but I did have a lot of respect for him and how he did things. He was straight-up and strong with his. They're lucky I didn't choose Suge because he would have found a way to break all deals. But I knew there was no way that Cheryl would be going for that, so again there would be no Pepa without Salt and vice versa.

Louis was a godsend. He wasn't trying to steal us away. He just wanted to help. And that was Hurby and Carol's worse nightmare come true. Hurby and Carol tried to keep the reins on me. But I ran the streets and partied with people too much. Hurby used to try to tell me not to go out. He would try to degrade me by saying, "Everybody thinks you're a slut, Sandra! You're making the group look bad."

He used to really rip me up. He knew where to hit me.

"People think you have no class, Sandra," he would say. "You need to tone it down."

I knew I was rough, but he was going too far. And I wasn't

out there screwing around like that. I knew it was just a tactic to try to control me. He was trying to hit me where he thought it would hurt. It did hurt, but not enough for me to stop pushing to get us more money and a better deal. I wouldn't stop until I got it.

Finally, I got Cheryl to listen. And Hurby and Carol caved in, too. They knew we were about to negotiate a new deal, and it would be easy for us to bring in new management and they didn't want that. So they listened. They negotiated with us. They gave us more points and a better deal. They came to the table.

That move empowered me. It made me feel that I could handle my business. But more than that, it solidified me as part of this group. I knew, after that, they couldn't get rid of me. I would be Pepa forever.

CHAPTER ELEVEN

Somma Time Man: Tah Tah

SALT-N-PEPA WERE RIDING HIGH OFF the success of *A Salt with a Deadly Pepa,* with songs such as "Shake Your Thang" bringing the go-go movement all over the country. It was another platinum seller, and life was going pretty well. I had bought and moved into my first place—a condo in Jamaica Estates, a middle-class neighborhood near St. John's University. And as usual, I was looking for love. Actually, I wasn't looking for love, it just always seemed to find me when I least needed it. I wish I could have just focused on my career, but when I met Tah Tah, I got swept off my feet.

My sister Dawn used to bartend at this nightspot in Queens called the Red Parrot. I would drop in from time to time to hang out with Dawn and chill. One day, I had just bought a new gray Mercedes-Benz coupe and I wanted to show it off. I loved cars and always had one, and I was known around the neighborhood for my driving skills. Even today, I'm known in Queens and parts of Jersey for my driving skills. I started drag racing when I got my first car. Yes, I used to drag race in that rusted-out Datsun, and I would win in that thing, too. Cheryl could tell you quite a few stories because she was in the car a lot when some random dude would pull up next to us (my cars were known in the hood) on the Grand Central Parkway and roll down the window and challenge me.

"Oh, boy!" she would say, and make sure her seat belt was tight, and I would take off. I could not be beaten on the Grand Central Parkway—the more traffic, the better. It didn't matter what kind of car I was driving. I have beaten people in my broke-down Datsun, my Jeep Wrangler, and of course my Mercedes. No one was willing to take the chances I was willing to take on the highway. Anyone racing me, especially in highway traffic, would eventually have to put on his brakes, and that's when he would lose. I had no fear, and there was no chance that I wouldn't take. I guess I felt invincible, as if I couldn't get in an accident. Thank God, I never did.

Guys would either be impressed by my driving skills or they would get punked. One guy was such a sore loser that he embarrassed himself in front of his boys. He and I were hanging out in this club in the city, and he challenged me to race to a specific destination in New Jersey. Whoever got to this place first would win a large sum of money. I should have had this sucker put up his money first.

I knew a shortcut, but I also did about 130 miles an hour on the New Jersey Turnpike and beat him there. But he refused to pay me. Now, we had made this bet in front of a bunch of people, and they all knew that I beat him, but he still wouldn't pay up. He said he didn't have it on him. But I knew he was just a sore loser. What a punk. But some guys got turned on by my driving. Tah Tah was one of those guys.

I met him at the Red Parrot the day I brought my new Mercedes by to show my sister Dawn. I was at the bar talking with Dawn when I noticed this guy staring. The first thing I noticed was how cute he was. He had a smooth, brown complexion with a neat, faded haircut. He was well dressed, in an expensive sweat suit, with new kicks. But his swagger was what got me. He came over to me with all of this confidence, as if he just knew I was going to talk to him. I was a little famous by now, and I wasn't really trying to talk to any strange men in a bar. But he had this way about him.

"What are you drinking?" he asked when he came over.

Before I could answer, he said, "As a matter of fact, I'm buying for everybody. Hey, everybody, drinks are on me!"

The bar was packed. And people started cheering. I found out later that he did that just to impress me. It worked. He told me he recognized me and wanted me to know that he could more than hold it down. I could tell that he was somebody. Not only could he afford to buy everybody a drink, but also I noticed how much respect he got from the other people in the bar. Everybody seemed to know him, and when certain dudes came in, they made it their business to come over to give him a pound and say hello. I had asked my sister who he was even before he came over. He stood out.

"Oh, that's Tah Tah," she said, as if to tell me everybody knew him.

Tah Tah spent the rest of the night making me laugh and trying to get me to go out with him. He was cute but I was playing it cool, as I always did. I wouldn't give him my number. I left and didn't come back to the bar for a few days. But my sister kept me informed: "Tah Tah wants to talk to you. He keeps bugging me for your number."

I was playing hard to get. I was Pepa from Salt-N-Pepa. I couldn't just be giving out my number like that. I came back to the Red Parrot a couple more times and still didn't give him my number or much play. But he was persistent. Finally, I broke down and we went on a date.

Everything between us happened so quickly. I was attracted to him from the first time I saw him, even though I wouldn't let him know it. But after our first date, it was done. Love was in the air, at least for me. What I loved about him was his swagger. Most guys I went out with during this time were caught up in me being Pepa. He didn't seem to care that I was Pepa. Most guys were all up in my grill and wouldn't give me space to breathe. They were possessive and jealous. Tah Tah had his own world and his own life that didn't have anything to do with me, and he had no problem telling me that he had stuff to do. I liked that . . . in the beginning.

The last thing I wanted was a man who would be so caught up with me that he would get in the way of my career. I never had that problem with Tah Tah.

Yes, he was a street hustler. And you would think I would have learned my lesson with Tommy. But I guess you attract what you're around. Rap and hip-hop attract a certain element. There weren't many CEO types or Wall Street dudes hanging out on the road on tour or at the concerts or the after parties. There weren't many men in Brooks Brothers suits in my neighborhood. And if there were, I simply wasn't seeing them. But to be honest, even if one of those guys had approached me, I probably wouldn't have given him much of my time. Not back then. I was a thrill seeker, and these street guys were edgy and scary and fun. Something about the street guys turned me on. Tah Tah had a lot of thrill with him.

As I mentioned, I was legendary on the roads in Queens. I couldn't be beaten on a race along the Grand Central Parkway or down Linden Boulevard. Tah Tah had heard about my driving skills and decided to put me to the test. Don't ever dare me to do something, because it's on. So he bet me that he could beat me from Alston's, this bar we were hanging out in on Liberty Avenue, to the Crowne Plaza Hotel near La Guardia Airport. I knew that whoever hit the Van Wyck Expressway first was going to win. He had a sporty BMW 3-Series, and I had my Mercedes coupe. We were neck and neck down Liberty Avenue. Heading onto the Van Wyck, the road merges from two lanes into one for the on-ramp. There isn't enough room for two cars. I knew that road well and knew that I could get to that merge before him. All I needed to be was ahead by a nose and it was mine. He was flooring it and so was I. And when we hit the merge, I was slightly ahead of him and gunned it. He tried to squeeze through and ended up banging his car against the concrete guardrail and spun out onto the Van Wyck. He banged his car up pretty well. And, of course, I beat him to the hotel.

He hated to lose to me, but the race was exciting and his adrenaline was pumping and so was mine. It was a good thing we were in front of a hotel. Tah Tah talked about that race for years.

"What was I thinking!" he said, about coming onto that ramp like that. He couldn't believe he'd messed his car up and couldn't believe that I'd put the squeeze on him forcing him into that guardrail. That race sealed our relationship. It shaped what would be this whirlwind, crazy ride, a roller-coaster relationship.

Tah Tah introduced me to gambling. He loved to gamble and taught me how to play cee-lo and blackjack. On the streets, he was known for his dice game the way I was known for my driving. If you played Tah Tah, you were going to lose. He had a magic about him when it came to those dice and those cards. He took me to Las Vegas a few times and he always won. One time he walked away with $90,000 at the blackjack table.

Tah Tah was a winner. He had his own business. You know every street hustler back then had them a business, whether it was a sneaker spot or a corner store or a nightclub. Tah Tah had a sneaker spot, he had his own car, his own money, and his own place. I had my place in Jamaica Estates, but he never wanted to live with me, which many men wanted. I liked that, too.

At this time, I was kind of feeling myself, my stardom. I was cocky. I ruled over any man that I was with. I always got my way. But not with Tah Tah. He wasn't sweating me. I was used to locking a man down. No one ever left me. I was the one doing the leaving. I was the one making the rules. When I said, "Let's chill, let's hang out," that's what would happen. Tah Tah would easily say, "Nah, I have something to do." And he would go. I had to practically beg him to spend time with me.

And because Tah Tah wouldn't let me run all over him, it made me want him even more. I wasn't in control of him, and it bothered me as much as it made me want him. I became obsessed with him. I wanted to be with Tah Tah every day, every waking moment. I was completely sprung, which wasn't at all my style.

I ended up getting pregnant. I hadn't planned on getting pregnant. It was inconvenient considering all of the things I was doing. Hurby didn't take it well. During my pregnancy he cut my pay and would restrict my participation in shows. We had a new album out that was burning up the charts. *Blacks' Magic* had "Expression," which was blazing, and Hurby wrote this song "Let's Talk About Sex," which would solidify Salt-N-Pepa as icons in rap. But at this time, all I was thinking about was Tah Tah and having his baby.

As I mentioned, I came from an old-fashioned, traditional family. My mother and father were married and were together with all of us kids. My sisters got married before having their babies. That's what you were supposed to do. You got married and you had children. Now here I am pregnant. I'm having this man's baby and I just knew we were going to get married. Of course, we were going to get married because I was having his baby, and that's just what you did. I was so excited that I couldn't wait to tell him. I went over to the Red Parrot, which was where he could be found every day. I walked in, and there he was holding court at the far end of the bar, and I just blurted it out.

"I'm pregnant!"

I was all smiling, expecting him to jump up and give me a huge hug and an "Oh, baby, I'm so happy! Let's get married or let's move in together. It's going to be just you and me and this baby!"

That's the picture I had in my mind. That this was it; it was settled. I was pregnant and he was my man and we would be a family. I really had this dream. Tah Tah and I would be together forever.

But that's not what happened. When I told him, he just sat there. He had no expression on his face and he gave me no reaction. I could see that not only was he *not* ready for my big announcement, but he also didn't like it. Boy, did he turn my world upside down.

After seeing his reaction, I put it on him strong. I wasn't having it.

"I'm pregnant and now we're going to be together, just you and me!" I started dictating to him how it was going to be.

I wanted a ring. I wanted us to get married. I laid it all down. He didn't say a word. So I figured I got through to him. He even showed up at my place one day with a ring. He was so funny. He came in with this box and said, "Here," and ran out of the room like a little kid who was nervous. I opened the box and saw this beautiful ring that I thought meant what a diamond ring means—that we were engaged. Later he would tell me it was just a friendship ring, that I had pressured him so much that he had to get me something. He didn't want to disappoint me and didn't want to tell me what he was really feeling—which was that he wanted out. He didn't want to be a father.

While I'm cherishing this ring and thinking that Tah Tah and I are going to get married, he grew more and more distant. And eventually, he stopped coming around.

I had to track him down. He wouldn't return my calls. He came around when he felt like it. And the more he dissed me, the more I went crazy trying to be with him.

Before the pregnancy everything was great: we traveled, we had fun, we hung out. After he found out I was pregnant, it all stopped. The next thing I knew I was hearing about some girl named Tasha. When you live in a neighborhood and you're from that neighborhood, everybody knows everybody. It's hard to step out and not have someone see you. But the way it got back to me, Tah Tah wasn't being discreet. Everybody seemed to know about him and Tasha.

I couldn't deal with it and didn't want to believe it. So I showed up one day at the Rucker in Harlem, where they held this basketball tournament every summer. Back then, a lot of street hustlers sponsored teams and they played one another. It was a big deal—NBA players played in this, top college players, and the best street ballers all represented. It was serious. And the park was always packed. I showed up to see one of Tah Tah's games, and this girl was right there with him. I could tell by their body language that they were together.

And I recognized her. I had seen her at different places around the neighborhood when Tah Tah and I were supposedly still together. She would be off to the side near him but seemingly by herself. She was one of those hood girls who were ghetto fabulous—the ones who always had nice clothes, nails done, and hair tight. But she never seemed to have a job. She was just always geared down, always dressed, and always taken care of.

Finally, I sat Tah Tah down. "Be real with me. Let me know the deal."

When I said that, he told me the deal. He told me, yes, he was seeing this girl Tasha, and his plan was to be with her. He wanted to break it off with me.

What?!

Here I am like four months pregnant with his baby, and it was like he kicked me in the stomach. And he was so nice about it. He wasn't mean or cruel. And I guess by hiding this thing he had with Tasha, he was trying to spare my feelings. But he also wasn't the type of guy to lie outright. So there it was. He didn't want to be with me anymore.

Guess what? I wasn't trying to hear that. He wasn't going anywhere, as far as I was concerned. I was having his baby, and he was going to be with me. So I pulled out all of the stops. I was going to try anything to win him back. I started talking to his sisters and going over to his mother's house. She was really in my camp. His poor mother wanted us to be together so badly and even tried to talk to Tah Tah.

I was obsessed and completely gone. I was trying anything to win him back. I knew that purple was his favorite color. And if I knew I was going to see him, I would make sure I had on a purple outfit. I even painted my nails purple and put his initials on my nails in rhinestones.

But nothing I did was working. And worse, he started showing up places publicly with Tasha on his arm, almost flaunting their relationship. It was embarrassing because I was a star running after this street dude who was publicly dissing me. My friends tried to talk me down off the ledge, but I was hardheaded. Cheryl would say, "Come on, Sandy. You have to move on." These were words I had spoken to her about Hurby. She didn't listen to me and I wasn't listening to her.

I could only see the possibilities—having his baby and living with him as a family—not the truth. I was ignoring the truth, which kept slapping me in the face.

Everywhere I went, it seemed, I was running into Tah Tah and Tasha. It was hard to not see him because we rolled in the same circles and frequented some of the same places. One night my sister Bev got me to go out with her to see a play, at the Beacon Theater in New York.

"Come on, Sandy, you *have* to get out of the house and do something," she said. "It will be fun."

I had been in the house for weeks just depressed and crying a lot. Bev was pregnant, too, and I hadn't hung out with her in a while, so I decided to go.

At intermission, my sister and I got on the elevator to go downstairs to get something to drink. As the doors opened, who was standing in front of us? Tah Tah and Tasha. They were lovey-dovey, arm in arm, cackling and enjoying themselves. I just stood there, stunned. Tah Tah saw the look on my face. We didn't speak.

But afterward he called me. He must have felt bad. And I was so happy for the attention. It gave me hope.

I started calling him to invite him to hang out with me. I was playing myself out so badly.

"Come on, Tah Tah, let's just go shoot some pool," I would tell him. "We don't have to do anything, but let's just hang out."

He wouldn't hang out. I kept calling him every day. Tasha answered the phone one time and said, "Look, stop calling him. You look really dumb. I'm sitting right here while you're begging him to play pool with you. He doesn't want you!"

"Yes, he does!" I screamed. "It's just a matter of time!"

I hung up on her. I was so mad. I was so hurt. I was so crazy and out of my mind. A few weeks later, somebody called me and told me that Tah Tah was at this club in Queens and had got shot. It was about two in the morning and I grabbed my coat and ran out of the house. Everybody was telling me not to go. Even my mother was trying to talk to me, but I wasn't listening to anyone. They all knew I was running right into some hurt. But I couldn't stop myself.

When I got to Jamaica Hospital, Tasha was sitting there with her friends and family. I could tell that my going there was a bad move. When they saw me, I could see they wanted to fuck me up. It was nothing for girls to jump another girl—even if she was pregnant—over some shit like this. I just knew I was going to get jumped right there. But I guess Tasha knew if she did, Tah Tah would be mad at her. So they held back. But if looks could kill . . .

A few of the nurses recognized me and I told them whom I was there to see. They pulled strings and got me in to see Tah Tah. I was the first person who got to see him. He had all of these tubes sticking out of him, but he was alive and awake.

"Are you okay?" I asked, and he nodded. I was thinking that he was happy to see me. Then Tasha came in and pushed past me to his bedside. He grabbed her hand and I was standing right there. It was killing me. He was looking at me like "Pep, let's stop doing this." I was just standing there looking stupid. He finally said to me, "I got to talk to her. You know . . . ," and he nodded for me to leave.

"Right. Right," I said. "Okay, well, I'm going to leave now. You take care of yourself."

I went home feeling like a piece of crap. I was crying and all messed up in the head. I wanted this man and I couldn't have him and I wasn't accepting that. A month or two before the baby was due, I got a little bit of hope. Tah Tah invited me to go to Vegas with him. He knew how much I loved to gamble, and he asked me to go. I hadn't stopped calling him and I was constantly begging him to hang out. So he finally said, "Yes." I was so happy. We were going to get back together was all I was thinking.

I paid for the room, and as we were checking out, I saw the phone bill. He spent practically the whole time on the phone talking to Tasha. I found out that she agreed to let him take me to Vegas as long as he didn't touch me. He kept his promise to her. I also found out that she was pregnant, too—just three months behind me.

This was a crazy time in my life. As I said, Salt-N-Pepa was in full force. We had "Expression" and, ironically, "Do You Want Me" and finally "Let's Talk About Sex" heating up the charts. Publicly, I am this star, part of this successful rap group. People are asking me for my autograph. I am performing (before I got too big to perform). I was cool, confident Pep on the outside. The chameleon blending in, showing the world only the good stuff. But on the inside, I was a total mess.

I know I was wearing Cheryl and Spin out with my drama. But we all managed to hold it together, as we always did. During this time, I met Gavin. Actually Spin and I met Gavin at a club. Gavin and I hit if off instantly. He was hanging with these guys who were trying to talk to Spin and me. Yeah, I still had it, even pregnant. Gavin's friends wanted to party, and he was kind of laid-back and didn't talk much. We all became friends and started hanging out. Gavin and I became so tight—partly because of how cool he was, his personality, but also because of the crazy things we went through (don't I always end up in some crazy situations?).

I was capitalizing on my fame and started hosting a night in Queens at this club, Crystals, near the Jamaica Avenue terminal. It was Pepa Night at Crystals and it was always packed. I always had a hustle. I would drop in early to show my face and mingle with the people, then I would come back at the end of the night to collect my money.

On this particular night Gavin and one of his boys were rolling with me. We pulled up in my new cherry-red Lexus coupe. When I got out, I noticed this dude standing in front of the club, but I didn't think much about him. We all went into the club. It was a few minutes before closing. I collected my money and Gavin and his friend left with me. They walked over to the passenger side, waiting for me to open the door, and this guy— the same guy I'd spotted when I was going in—came up and grabbed me and pushed this gun into the side of my head.

"Bitch, give me the keys," he said. "And don't nobody move or I will blow her fucking brains out!"

I hesitated. Instead of just giving him the keys, I started thinking, *How am I going to get home? This is a brand-new car. I'm not going to just give him my car!*

93

I didn't want to give him the keys.

"Yo, give me the keys!" he said, pressing the gun harder against my head. "Bitch, give me the keys!"

I was so mad. This was my car. I worked for it. I wasn't going to just give it to this bitch-ass thug, gun or no gun. I was way angrier than I was scared. But Gavin saw what was going down, and he had to speak up.

"Pep, please give him the keys."

I looked at Gavin and saw something in his eyes that told me that I should give this guy the keys or he would definitely kill me. So I gave him the keys and he pushed me away.

"Now, back the fuck up!" he said to Gavin and his friend.

Another car pulled up. They were strapped with guns by the window. The guy got in my car and drove off. I was so mad. Everything was in the car. He took my pocketbook, the few thousand dollars I'd just collected, and everything I had. We called the cops, and they came and took my statement and said, "We'll get in touch with you."

"I'm riding with you to find my car," I told them. I was still mad.

"Miss, you can't do that," the officer said. "We will call you when we find your car."

Oh, hell no! I was going with them to find my car. They ended up letting me ride with them. We rode around all night. We didn't find my car that night, but they did find my car the next day. Someone ran his mouth. They must have bragged about jacking Pepa for her car, and the cops found it before the thieves could ship it overseas, which was their plan.

I knew from that night that Gavin was cool under pressure. But he really showed himself one summer day. I was on Linden Boulevard and I had my baby, Tyran, in the backseat in his car seat. I saw Gavin near this park and I pulled over to talk to him. I got out of the car and we were standing there talking.

That week, this neighborhood guy had just gotten out of jail, and he went on a killing spree. He killed about ten people in a grocery store and was on the run. Now what were the odds of him being right where we were at the same time? And what were the odds of him coming up to me while I was standing there with Gavin and trying to jack my car to get away?

Well, that's what happened. The cops were looking for him. Helicopters were swirling around, and this murderer came up to me and tried to get into my car.

"No, no!" I started screaming. "Let me get my baby out, let me get my baby!"

I didn't care about the car, I wasn't going to let him drive off with my baby. He knocked me to the ground. This guy was big and buff, as if all he did in prison was lift weights. I was crying and screaming and trying to pull on this giant man to stop him from taking my car with my baby in it.

Gavin started cursing this guy out. "You pussy! You sucker-ass pussy! Hey, punk!" Gavin was trying anything to get this man to stop what he was doing, and it was working. His pride couldn't take Gavin calling him a pussy, and it was making him mad and Gavin kept breaking on him. He finally started going after Gavin.

"Pep, go, go!" Gavin screamed as soon as the man moved away from the car. I immediately jumped in, but I didn't want to pull off because I just knew this guy was going to kill Gavin.

The man stopped going after Gavin when he realized what was happening. But it was too late.

"Pep, go!" Gavin said.

I jumped in my car and pulled off. Gavin wasn't a fighter.

He was kind of skinny and he wasn't really a street dude. But he was quick thinking and saved my baby's life. I saw Gavin take off running. He might fake you out, but he never punks out. The murderer guy must have sensed that if he chased Gavin and beat him to death, there was a good possibility that he would get caught. So he decided to run in the other direction. They caught him a week later. But I will never forget Gavin for that, and I couldn't thank him enough.

We were really tight after that and I took him everywhere with me. I loved guys as friends. When you're not sleeping with them, men are the best. Gavin was the best of the best. I had told Cheryl all of these stories about him before they even met, and by the time they did meet, he was already a hero in her mind. I knew they would hit it off.

"I have the perfect person for you!" I told Gavin.

He, of course, knew who she was and was definitely eager to meet her. At the time, Cheryl had already dumped Hurby for the third time. She was going through her own drama dealing with that and a bunch of other stuff. Gavin was single, and I just thought they would make a perfect couple. I seemed to have vision for other people, but when it came to me, I was totally blind. They say that's how it is for people who have special gifts. But I could see that Gavin and Cheryl would work.

I was right. They more than hit it off. They ended up married!

For me, it wasn't so easy. While Cheryl was starting a new romance, I was still hoping to get back my old one. I figured that once the baby came it would be real for Tah Tah and he would come around and want to be my man again.

The day I went into labor, I called him. Tah Tah had promised to be in the delivery room with me, and he said he was coming right away to be with me. I tried to wait for him, but the contractions were fierce. I was in a lot of pain, and finally Cheryl went to the hospital with me. She was there the whole time. Tah Tah never showed up. I was so stressed-out and worried about Tah Tah not being there that I couldn't concentrate on delivering my baby. I was in labor for thirty-six hours. I couldn't dilate. I got a high fever. They had to perform a C-section.

Tah Tah didn't show up until the next day. By then I was out of it and sick and so was our baby.

We had a son and I named him Tyran, which was Tah Tah's real name. I named the baby Tyran partly because I wanted to solidify that connection to Ta-Ta. But I also did it to spite his girlfriend.

Yeah, bitch, I had his first son and he's got his name!

I was so crazy, wasn't I? Here I was using my baby to try to pay somebody back.

Tah Tah didn't come around even after the baby was born. I had the worse case of postpartum depression, too. I think I had just regular depression before the baby came, and it got a whole lot worse after I delivered my baby. I was stressed and sad and angry all at once. I had never been that depressed in my whole life. I can't explain why this hit me so hard. I don't know what it was about Tah Tah, but I just couldn't let him go.

After the baby came, I was still calling Tah Tah every day. If only he were a mean person. If he had just said, "Bitch, don't call me no more! It's over!" maybe I would have stopped. But he was nice.

I was trying everything to win him over. I even paid for him to train at Gleason's Gym in Brooklyn. He wanted to be a boxer, and I pulled some strings to get him a trainer at Gleason's. But Tah Tah got into a fight and ended up getting stabbed and couldn't train anymore. So that was money down the tubes.

I was just spiraling out of control. I was getting crazier and crazier over this man. One day he came to me and asked for money. He told me he needed $25,000 for this store he wanted to get. Now mind you, he hadn't shown up any other time, hadn't spent much time with me or our baby, and now he wants money? I was going to give it to him. I told him if he wanted the money, though, he would have to come over and hang out.

"Don't send your boy to get it," I told him. "*You* have to come."

I was desperate. He said he would come over and get it and hang out. I had the check ready for him. He called and said he would be over around three in the afternoon the next day. Three o'clock came and went, and I got a call around five, telling me that he was on his way.

I called one of my girlfriends around seven when he didn't show up. I was crying hysterically.

She tried to console me: "Maybe he got caught up or something. He will be there."

When I got off the phone, I got on my knees and prayed. "Please, God, if he doesn't come here tonight, by tomorrow morning when I open my eyes, please take the feeling that I have for him away from me!"

All of this time I had been praying to God for Tah Tah to love me, for him to be with me. I had never prayed to *not* love him.

I cried until I thought every ounce of water was drained out of my body. I couldn't cry anymore and I wanted that feeling in the pit of my stomach to go away. I fell asleep and in the morning he still hadn't come. When he finally rang my bell around noon the next day, I felt something different inside. Usually, I would have butterflies just at the thought of seeing him. I used to lose my breath. Has anyone ever felt that way over a person? Crazy, isn't it?

I would just want to jump on him and kiss him and tell him I loved him. This time, however, I felt nothing. I didn't want to trust it until I saw him. When I got to the door and opened it, I felt nothing. He came in and I was standing there holding his check. I looked at him and it made me nervous because of what I was *not* feeling. I thought I was bugging.

"You know, you're not getting this," I said, finally breaking the silence.

"Whatever, Pep," he said.

"Yeah, whatever, motherfucker!" I ripped up the check into a thousand little pieces and threw them at him. In all of this time, through all of our shit, I had never cursed at him. I had never even uttered a harsh word at him. But this time was different.

He left my house mad as hell. About an hour later my phone rang. It was him. He wanted to tell me off.

"Forget you!"

"Forget you!" I shot back. "You ain't shit!"

I told him everything I never thought I was thinking about him. And when I was finished breaking on him, I hung up. I couldn't believe all of the stuff that was coming out of my mouth. I sat in my room for a second real still. I had to ask myself, "Do you want him?" The answer was no. I didn't want him. That feeling was gone, was really gone, and it never came back.

Months after this, Tah Tah tried to come back. And believe me, I would have loved to have taken him back. My dream of the happy family was still there buried somewhere. I would have loved to be with my son's father and for us to be happy. But I truly wasn't feeling Tah Tah like that anymore.

We did, however, end up being friends, or at least on good terms. He told me that I must have had some sort of witchcraft on him. He remembered that day—that last day, which was my last straw. And he told me every time he tried to get to my house something kept happening to keep him from me. He couldn't explain it, but he felt that a force was stopping him. And when I ripped up that check and threw him out, something happened to him. Things just weren't going right for him after that. He wanted me back, but it was too late. I had moved on. And I never looked back.

To this day, he still keeps in touch with my family, and he even talks to my mom. I learned that Tyran talks to him frequently, too, which I think is great.

Tah Tah is in jail (at the time of this book). He got tangled up in some mess involving Murder Inc. and Irv Gotti and the drug dealer Supreme and was sent away for first-degree murder, but he got out of those charges and they got him for conspiracy or something. To tell you the truth, I don't know the details. I don't want to know. I didn't want to get sucked into all of that. I do know that rapper 50 Cent named Tah Tah in a record as one of the people that might have shot him all of those times. I don't know about all of that, either. What I do now know is that Tah Tah wasn't right for me. I just couldn't see it then.

I look back on that time as one of my craziest, and I never want to be like that over a man again. Ever. Not that I didn't make some horrible choices after Tah Tah, because I did. With Tah Tah, we just weren't in the same place. He was young and into his game, and he needed to be in control. I was established and wanted to settle down. I had a career and my own money, and a dude like that at his age wanted a chick who needed him, whom he could be *the man* with.

I also know that I came on kind of strong. I never had a man who didn't cater to me and didn't do what I wanted. And I wanted to conquer him. I wasn't in a place to really know what love was or what it was supposed to look like. I thought I loved Tah Tah, but I really just wanted to control him.

How do you learn about love when you've never seen it? I had no guidance. My parents weren't real lovey-dovey. They were both busy trying to feed this big family. So I didn't see the kind of fairy-tale love you read about or see in the movies. What I wanted was the fairy tale, which I never got to see.

For me, love was about pain. I felt that if a man cursed at me or hit me, he must love me. If I could get him that mad, then he must really love me. Tah Tah never did those things, so I wanted to make him love me. I could never get him that mad (not that I ever purposefully did that to a man), so he must not have cared.

So I didn't know what love was. I had no guidance but the streets. And the streets ain't no place to learn about love.

As a mother of a son, I have made sure to school my son about how to talk to women and how to treat women. I would never let him hit a girl. I taught him that real men don't hit. I wouldn't even let him play rough with his sister. Girls are to be treasured, I taught him. At least my son knows better, and I know he will do better. I think parents have to talk about these things with their sons and daughters. They have to let their daughters know that it's not okay for a man to put his hands on them. It's not okay to be abused. You have to teach your daughter that she is a precious treasure worthy of being treated like a gem, because she is.

No one ever told me that. I had to learn that lesson the hard way.

CHAPTER TWELVE

Partying like Rock Stars

AFTER I RECOVERED FROM MY craziness with Tah Tah, I was ready to party. It was as if a veil had been lifted and I could see again. I got over my depression and started living. Tyran was one thing that got me out of it. He was such a sweet baby, and I loved him so much. I had too much to live for just looking into his little face every day. I was caught up in being a mother. And I was caught up in being a rap star.

I was completely back to my old self—partying like there was no tomorrow.

We had a huge hit with *Black's Magic*. We had gone platinum . . . again. There were more tours, more attention, more videos, more money. There was more opportunity to have fun. I didn't go completely back to my old ways, though. I had given up a few things, including drugs. Not that I was ever big into them. But I did enjoy smoking a few coolies in my day. I quit smoking when I found out I was pregnant and didn't look back. That was how it was for me. Once I decided to do something, I was done.

Cheryl and I were fortunate. When we were coming up, everybody was doing some kind of drugs. Everybody was smoking weed. You had groups such as Cypress Hill whose whole thing was smoking weed. A lot of rappers didn't believe you could write dope rhymes unless you had been high on weed. And of course there was cocaine. It was nothing for us to walk into a party in someone's house and or even at certain clubs and see trays of whatever you wanted—cocaine, marijuana, you name it. It was just the norm, and everybody seemed to be doing it. It wasn't taboo and there wasn't a stigma attached to using drugs. And I tried just about everything—even cigarettes.

People didn't seem to be getting strung out back then, either—not until crack came into the picture and that got deep. I had to watch my sister Dawn go through that, and it was painful. I watched her go from this tough fly girl whom I could depend on for anything to a crack addict. That crack ruined a lot of lives.

But when Salt-N-Pepa were coming up, the drug scene was different. We were on the road when we were first introduced to cocaine. We didn't snort it; someone, a rap veteran, gave us a cigarette laced with cocaine. They called them coolies and we smoked them. We used to smoke coolies pretty often.

I remember us smoking it and Cheryl bugging. She was worse than I was when she was high. (I guess it was because I was pretty out there all of the time anyway.) Cheryl would get this crazy look on her face and get paranoid. One time the fire alarm went off in our hotel and she panicked because she thought we were going to get in trouble. "Cheryl, it's just a drill," I tried to calm her down. "We didn't pull the alarm. It's just a drill and we have to leave."

But she swore that we did it and we were going to get into trouble and refused to leave. Cheryl didn't smoke many coolies after that. We never made it a habit. We drank, we partied, we were having the time of our lives. But we didn't get hooked on anything! And thank God, we didn't keep doing it.

Hurby was having fun, too. The more success we had, the bigger his head got. He would come up with more ideas for new songs, and he had us working harder than ever on writing lyrics for these songs, working on dance moves for our stage shows and videos. He was getting more and more loose with his other women, too, which was driving Cheryl crazy. Everyone knew. Everyone was afraid to say anything to Cheryl. But she wasn't going to leave. I knew talking to her straight-up about it would only cause us to fall out. Besides, Hurby might actually follow through on his threat and replace me. I knew Cheryl wasn't ready to leave.

I understood firsthand. I was going through various relationships at the same time—some of them worse than what Cheryl was dealing with. And I knew there was nothing a person could say to me to make me leave. When you think you're in love, you will put up with things that you would never put up with if you were in your right mind. Feeling like that is definitely like being crazy. I was crazy for my son's father like that. I was completely out of my mind for him. And nothing my mother, my sisters, Cheryl, my other friends, or anyone could have said to me would have made me move on and leave him alone. Nothing.

So I just tried to be there for Cheryl until she was ready. I would say to her, "Can you move on? Can you just get past it?"

And she wouldn't say anything. She would just be miserable and take it. I know those experiences made it easy for her to walk away from Salt-N-Pepa when she did. I know her memories of being in the business aren't what mine are. We were definitely living different lives.

Despite that, Cheryl was like my sister. She was one of my biggest encouragers and supporters. We were together so much and went through so many things together. We even fought like sisters. Thank God it never got that serious. We never came to blows. Cheryl says if that had ever happened, if we had ever had a fistfight, we probably couldn't be close today. That would have been something she couldn't have gotten past. I don't know. But I'm glad it never happened. We did come close, though.

I have this thing where I hate to be the brunt of a joke. I don't like people laughing at me. Maybe it goes back to the days when my father used to call me a dunce. I don't like people ridiculing me, calling me names, and I don't like to be the victim of a joke. I don't like to be embarrassed. I know no one likes it. But I really lose it when it happens. I'm a bit more mature today. But back then, there was no stopping me.

Cheryl and I were on tour with Ice-T and a bunch of other acts. As usual, we were the only girls. We were all hanging out and Cheryl said something, I don't even remember what. But I know whatever she said, I thought she was making fun of me, and everyone was laughing. I was eating some grapes at the time, and when I looked around and saw everyone laughing at me, I spit my whole mouthful of grapes in Cheryl's face.

I remember her picking them off her face, and I was standing there looking at her like *What?!* waiting for her to do something. Cheryl didn't say anything like *Bitch, what's your problem?* She just said, "I can't believe you spit grapes in my face."

I was so emotional. I just did it. There was nothing to say. I was hot. I'm not proud of it. I remember her sliding the grapes mess off her face. It was amazing how they just stuck there. It stopped the laughter, though.

I loved Cheryl for just moving on. You know how you fight with your family and it can be really bad, but somehow you manage to still love each other. You can move on as if nothing ever happened. That's the way Cheryl and I were. She understood me. And I understood her.

Cheryl never made fun of me again after the grape-spitting incident. But I blew up like that a few other times, and people started to get the message not to put me in that situation. Chris (Play) was always joking around and snapping on people. We toured with Kid N Play early on. Hurby was their manager and produced *2 Hype,* their first album. We were hanging out at Denny's after a show and Play tried to clown me at the table. About fifteen of us were sitting at this long table. He said what he said, and of course everyone started laughing. I got up and grabbed him by his collar and dragged him down the whole length of the table, knocking everybody's food and drink onto the floor.

Cheryl had picked up her food and drink when she saw me get up because she knew there was going to be trouble. Play never made fun of me again.

People got used to me tripping. You travel so much with people and they become like your family. It's inevitable that when you spend so much time with people that they will eventually get on your nerves and vice versa. We used to argue and fight and fuss, but when it came time to do a show or record an album, we brought it all together.

As cool as Dee Dee and I were, we would get into it from

time to time, too. Our fights were mostly over dumb things such as clothes. As Dee Dee got more comfortable, she started doing things to get on my nerves. It was like having an annoying little sister, which I never had. Stylists would bring clothes and shoes and accessories for us to select for a show, and Dee Dee and I wore the same size clothes and shoes. Cheryl was petite and short. Dee Dee and I were about the same height and size. She would always get to the clothes first and pick the best stuff, leaving me with the scraps. Now here I am Pepa of Salt-N-*Pepa* and I have to pick over scraps? I wasn't some background person. I should have gotten first dibs on everything. I didn't think I should have to wake up super early just to beat her there (and everyone knew about my trouble with being places on time). She should have waited. But she didn't think she had to.

I usually didn't say anything and just let it go. I figured I didn't want to whip this girl's ass and have her leave the group, and then we wouldn't have a deejay and Hurby would be threatening me. So I let it slide a lot. But one time, I had enough. We had an appearance and once again Dee Dee got to the clothes first. I knew ahead of time what was coming, and I had my eye on these sneakers. I got down there late, of course, and there was Dee Dee with my sneakers.

I lost it. "Dee Dee, you're going to have to hand those over."

"No!" she said.

"Those are mine."

She wasn't trying to hear that. She put them on her feet.

"I'm about to count to motherfucking three, and you better get them off or I'm going to take them off!" I was serious. But she was holding on and wasn't budging.

"Okay, I'm giving you to three." I started getting ready, taking off my earrings. I was a little rough around the edges back then. No couth. I hadn't thought it through. I was just mad, hot.

"One," I started.

Cheryl knew what would happen if I got to three. She jumped in and stopped things:

"Please give Pep those sneakers!"

It must have clicked to Spin then that I was dead serious, and she gave me those sneakers. We kissed and made up that time. We always did. One time, though, our relationship almost didn't survive.

Dee Dee and I got caught up in some mess when she was married to former NBA basketball star Kenny Anderson. I used to rent out a night at this pool hall in Manhattan. It was a high-roller thing and I charged a cover of $50 just to get in. I used my celebrity to get people to come out and gamble, and I did pretty well. Everybody wanted to play on my table, which had a $500 fee just to get on. Kenny Anderson used to come there with his boys, and he would flirt with me. He would get to drinking and try to grab on me. My friends would be there and see him and ask, "Isn't that Spin's man? What's he doing?"

He was trying to kiss me and kept asking me to go for a walk with him. I kept pushing him away and he kept coming.

This put me in an awkward situation. Should I tell Spin? Hell no, I wasn't going to tell her. I knew I wouldn't let him cross the line, and I chalked it up to his drinking, so I let it go. Why stress her out about it? One time we were all in the club together and he started with that flirting stuff again. This time Spin must have seen him. After that she started throwing some stinkness my way. Her friends were throwing some shade, too.

It's really hard to work with someone who has an attitude with you. This went on for a while until I finally decided to confront Spin. We were on a plane heading to Los Angeles for an appearance and I said, "I noticed you have been a little chilly toward me lately. What's up?"

She told me that Kenny had told her that I had been coming on to him, and he said she should watch out for me. *Watch out for me?!* I couldn't believe it. He must have figured that he would throw it onto me because he was already busted. So he twisted it. And she believed him.

The stinkness between Spin and me went on for a while until she busted him cheating on her with other women and his drinking had got out of hand and she had a whole bunch of drama with him. Then she and I were cool again. We eventually always made up.

I wasn't somebody who went out of her way to bother anyone. I didn't like trouble, although I always seemed to be in the middle of some. What I wouldn't do, though, is, if trouble came to me, I wouldn't run from it. Another time, we were on the road with UTFO and we were at the bar in our hotel. We were all drinking and having fun. So why did one of the UTFO members want to start in on me? I do not know, but I wasn't having it. He was singling me out saying stuff. I had been drinking Long Island ice teas out of this giant mug, and I had knocked back a couple of them. So not only was I not going to let him clown me, but I was feeling kind of nice from the ice teas.

Cheryl was trying to calm it down. But this guy was being an asshole and wouldn't stop.

"You don't even want to mess with me," I told him. I felt that I was going to explode inside and would haul off and slap him if he kept it going. I'm sure he would have fought me back because of the kind of guy he was. But I didn't care. I was two seconds from slapping him when instead I decided to flip the table we were all sitting at.

Everybody's drink came crashing to the ground. My mug of Long Island ice tea was full. It flipped into the air and landed on the floor facedown without a drop of liquor spilling. Everybody stopped and looked. Glasses were broken and the floor was wet, and in the middle of it was my drink upside down still full.

Everyone was bugging. Cheryl looked at me because stuff like that happened all the time around me, and I know she would have sworn that I made that happen that way. But I didn't. I wasn't thinking about flipping that mug and making it land like that. It just happened. That mug scared people and made them want to leave the bar. I heard people went back to their rooms and tried to make that trick happen, but they couldn't.

I was wild, ghetto, and unaware. I wasn't thinking about being a role model then. To be honest, that didn't click with me until we did "Let's Talk About Sex," and I started to see how much one song could change lives. So many women came up to us and said how much we inspired them to be strong, how we got them thinking about sex and what they could get away with in relationships.

I didn't realize how big a deal that song was until we got a call from Peter Jennings. He was a big-time newsman on ABC. Apparently his daughter was a big fan of Salt-N-Pepa's and she had been listening to "Let's Talk About Sex." He asked her what she was listening to and she played it for him. When he heard the lyrics, he got an idea. Peter Jennings was a big AIDS activist and wanted to bring awareness about this disease that was killing so many people. He contacted our management and asked them if we would do a version of our song and make a PSA. We rewrote "Let's Talk About Sex" and came up with

"Let's Talk About AIDS," and we shot a video for it that his people paid for.

That was a big deal, and I know it went a long way toward making people—especially young people—aware of HIV and AIDS and other sexually transmitted diseases. I was proud of both songs. This was before TLC came out with their song with the condoms and making safe sex an issue. Salt-N-Pepa were first.

I wish someone had come out with a song like ours before us. I needed to hear that message and I needed to be more aware and informed. I ended up walking away from a relationship because of ignorance about HIV and AIDS.

November 7, 1991. That was the day Magic Johnson stood before the world and announced that he was HIV-positive. That announcement rocked me to my core. Back then, all anybody knew was that if you had HIV, you had AIDS, and if you had AIDS, you were going to die this horrible, nasty death where you would waste away to nothing with sores all over your body. That was what we knew. And nobody wanted to get AIDS. I also knew you caught AIDS from either drug use from a needle or through sex.

At the time I was in a relationship with an NBA basketball player, Derrick Coleman. He played for the New Jersey Nets and was a star.

I met him at Nell's, this nightclub in Manhattan. I was hanging out with Janet Jackson at the time. She was so cool. When she was in town, she would call me and we would we meet at a club and party all night. Janet loved to dance and party, and you know how I love to party. She was with Rene at the time, and I remember he wouldn't let her out of his sight. So I was there with Janet and Rene and I saw this tall, handsome guy from across the room. I didn't know who he was, I just knew he was tall. He figured I must be somebody because I was hanging out with Janet Jackson. He came over and started talking to me and we exchanged numbers.

Derrick Coleman was good to me. He was my baby. He wasn't like any of the men I was used to dating. He wasn't a thug and he wasn't very street. He was a real man but he was nice and gentle and respectful. So why did I go and mess that up? I blame Magic Johnson. After he made that announcement about having HIV, I started putting two and two together. I know it was so dumb of me. But I was thinking that Derrick was a ballplayer, and I'd heard that those guys in the NBA all shared women and were loose sexually. There was Wilt Chamberlain talking about his twenty thousand women. And now Magic talking about HIV and AIDS.

Derrick had never given me any indication that he was that type of dude. I just put him in that category. He was a baller and that was what ballers did. And I was scared of that. I didn't want to catch anything. So I started asking him to wear a condom. He wasn't having that. So I started making excuses for why I didn't want to see him. I stopped coming around and taking his calls. I was bugging out. And I couldn't quite explain it to him.

I tried to work with it. I was buying him colorful condoms and condoms with the bumps on them, condoms that heated up. I was trying to get creative to get him to wear them. But when he wouldn't wear a condom, I was through.

I panicked. Years later, look at Magic. All alive and healthy. And Derrick went on to be happy and I always wondered what-if. Had I stayed with Derrick, I would never have been with Brad. Derrick was one of those happily-ever-after kind of men. He was rich, he was confident. He was his own man. He wasn't going anywhere and would always have treated me well. I messed that up over something silly. I traded in a man who would been down for me until the end. And I ended up with Brad.

CHAPTER THIRTEEN

Naughty by Nature

IT WAS APRIL OF 1991 and Salt-N-Pepa was one of the headliner groups at MTV's Daytona Beach Spring Break. A couple of other groups were invited, including Cypress Hill and Naughty by Nature. As much as I was an artist, I was also a fan, and I loved Naughty by Nature. Actually, I loved that song "O.P.P."

I remember when it first came out, I was asking, "Who is that group?" I was especially interested in the guy who was talking about "splittin' and co-hittin' that." I mean who talked like that? That song was so hard and so nasty, but I loved it and wanted to know who performed it. They sounded cute.

I wanted to see if the face matched the voice, and I had gotten tickets to see Naughty by Nature at the Palladium in Manhattan. But on the night of the concert, the show was canceled. I was so disappointed. Then I found out that they were going to be at MTV's Spring Break with us. Finally, I would get to see them perform. I didn't know them, I just loved their music.

The first day in Daytona Beach, we're all there and we introduced ourselves to one another, and I was right, that guy who was talking "splittin' and co-hittin' " *was* cute. It was like at first sight.

I was there with my little boy, Tyran, who was almost two years old. I brought him with me because the show was at a theme park and I thought it would be fun. I was there to have fun, but I got a little bit more than I expected.

We had a couple of days to play before we had to perform, and we were enjoying the rides and the sun. I don't know how it all happened, but someone dared me to go on this bungee-jumping "ride" that they had. The "ride" was on a crane that was a hundred feet in the air with a bungee cord dangling from the end. You had to climb up the crane and they would strap you in. If you dare me to do something, I will do it. I will never punk out on a dare. So everyone was getting all hyped, and the dare was thrown down and I took it. And then Brad, whom I had just met earlier, was like "I got this! If she's going up there, I'm doing it, too!"

He was all gangsta with it. I was bold and said I would go first. I'll admit that when I got up there and looked over and saw nothing but the ground, I had second thoughts. This was back in the day when bungee jumping was dangerous. This was before they had worked out all of the kinks, and a few people had died doing it. I knew for sure that sucker wasn't regulated, it had be at least twenty feet higher than they allow today. But they dared me and I wasn't punking out.

Mommy and Daddy back in the day. This photo survived the fire
at the Anderson Road house.

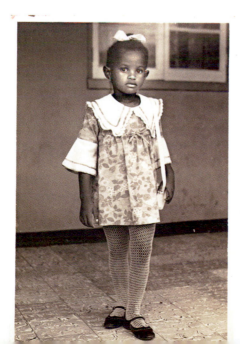

This is me in Jamaica,
age six. Now can you
see why I was destined
for stardom?

Ballet and
tap lessons
in Queens.

Graduating from IS 59.
My father was there,
proud.

First album publicity photo. Yes, the spandex and African Kinte hats were our own style. This is what people knew to be the Salt-N-Pepa look.

SALT - N - PEPA Fan Club Info:
Idolmakers, Inc.
P.O. Box 85
E. Elmhurst, NY 11369

Me and Tommy. This is the only photo of us that I have. We made a cute couple, huh?

Me and Prince Markie
D. I was sick with a
cold, but he made it
all better.

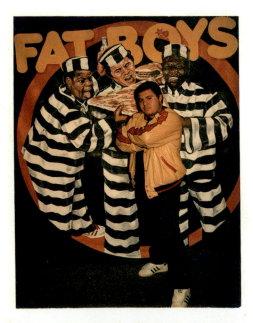

My Fat Boy.
Prince Markie D.

Me and Tah Tah and Tyran.
One big happy family?

Me and Tah Tah.
See, I have on his
favorite color, purple.

My crush, L.L. If only he . . . oh, well.

Another big happy family—me, Egypt, Brad.

It's official! We're married now! This was the wedding my mother wanted.

The three of us chilling in Miami during an interview.

This is me being naughty.

"Shoop" promotion photo. Yeah, Adele, no meat and potatoes now! We are slim and trim.

Me onstage rocking the mic! This is in Russia on tour with Ed Lover and a bunch of Russian acts.

It's nothing but a "She Thing."
This is a shot from our video.

Here we are on Grammy night.
We won! But we didn't get the
actual award until weeks later.
Oprah had us running in a race
the next day.

New York's finest! This is from the "She Thing" video. We're hot!

Salt-N-Pepa and En Vogue. This is from the "Whatta Man" video shoot.
We didn't get to perform together live until many years later.

My main man, my son, Tyran, age seventeen.

Me and my baby girl, Egypt. This is just after my nose job, so it's a little swollen.

Me bottle-feeding my baby, Frenchi̥ (don't forget the heart over the "i̥"!).

Hip Hop Honors—Queen Latifah's talking about how Salt-N-Pepa were pioneers.

Me and Adele Givens. She's the only comedienne that can talk about us. Instead of Salt-N-Pepa, we were "Meat-N-Potatoes." Funny.

Me and my girl Caprice at Prince Azim's (of Brunei) birthday party with actress Samantha Mumba.

Me and my surreal friends, Chyna Doll, Andrea Lowell, and Traci Bingham.

Me and Doug E. Fresh. His "The Show," led to our diss-record, "Show Stopper." He got over it. We're cool now.

Me and Gary Sheffield. Now why did I let this one get away?!

Yes, I'm hip hop but I love me some Tom Hanks! This is Grammy night.

Me and Cheryl, Puffy, Busta, and Brad—in Cancún chilling.

Ed Lover, Spin, me, Fab Five Freddy, and Cheryl—we're all pioneers of hip-hop.

My little boy was standing there and I could see that even he was scared for me. I kissed him and said, "Don't worry, Mommy will be okay." I got strapped in and took a deep breath. And I jumped. I didn't just jump, I had to do it backward just to show off. If I was going to do something that crazy, I had to do it with flair.

Then it was Brad's turn, and all that hard-core gangsta stuff went out the window. Homeboy was so scared I could see him shaking. But there was no way he was going to see me do my jump—backward, no less—and not go. So he did it. It was a crazy feeling to jump into thin air. I mean you felt you were jumping into nothing and were just free-falling. You felt as if you were certainly going to hit the ground and break every bone in your body and die, but then right before you reached the bottom, when all the air was out of your body and your stomach was nowhere to be found, that rope snapped your ass back up to safety. It was a crazy feeling—almost as if you had died and were brought back to life.

I know Brad must have felt like that because he was screaming, "Yeah! Yeah!" when he was done. The thug was back.

A lot of my relationships started on some crazy thrill, dare stuff. Maybe that should be a warning for me. Maybe my next relationship needs to start off on some real boring trip, some dinner-and-a-movie trip instead of drag racing and bungee jumping. Riding high off our surviving our bungee jumping, Brad and I hung out for the rest of the afternoon with our group.

I had to get back to my room to rest because Salt-N-Pepa was performing later that afternoon, and we were planning on flying back home that evening. Brad and I went back to the hotel, and we ended up in the elevator by ourselves. My room was on the tenth floor and his was on the eight. He asked me what I was doing after the show. I told him that we were flying back home.

"Why don't you stay," he said. "We perform tomorrow. Why don't you stay and hang out until the weekend."

I had my child with me and couldn't see staying a few extra days for a man I had just met. I didn't answer him because I was thinking. The elevator doors opened to his floor. He started to leave, but he turned around and came back and kissed me.

Fireworks went off in my head. I mean he had the softest, most juicy lips I had ever felt. That brother could kiss. And I kissed him back.

Now, I have no points on my license in the industry, meaning despite what Hurby tried to say, I was not known for giving it up like that. I had a clean driving record. I liked to party and I liked to have fun, but I've never been promiscuous—especially not with industry dudes. Prince Markie D was it until Brad.

When I got to my room, my stylist, Elena, who is also one of my best friends, was there.

"Girl, Brad just kissed me in the elevator," I said, beaming. "And he wants me to stay until the weekend. I can't do that, can I?"

I wasn't asking her permission, but I think I wanted her to tell me, *Girl, you must be crazy. Take your behind home!* But she said, "Sure, why not?"

"Well, I have Tyran. What am I going to do with him for two days?"

"I'll take him home with me."

"Really?"

"Sure!"

It was settled. I was staying. *What was I doing?* I was scared to stay. But I also figured that too many industry people and MTV folks were around for anything bad to happen to me. So I stayed.

I finally got to see Naughty by Nature perform, and I got to know Anthony Criss, aka Brad, a whole lot better.

It was a great time. He was so spontaneous and cool. We spent the next few days partying and talking. And the thing that I loved was that he didn't try to sleep with me. We kissed some more, but that was as far as that went.

I guess he respects me, I thought to myself.

I wasn't some chicken head or groupie. I wasn't some regular chick. I was an established artist, too. Salt-N-Pepa was huge. And he respected that and treated me as special.

By the time we got back to New Jersey, we were inseparable. Being with him was like that bungee-jump ride—it was scary and thrilling, it took my stomach and gave me a rush all at the same time. I never knew what to expect from him, and that was both good and bad. I started to see the bad less than a month into our relationship.

We were at a party and I was being my bubbly self, mingling with the other guests. It was a party he brought me to in New Jersey. The thing was, Brad met me being the life of the party, bugging out and having fun, so I didn't think anything about mingling with the guests and being my crazy self. But he was upset. I later found out that he thought I was being a little too friendly. When I was ready to go, I went to find him and someone told me he had left.

"Left?!" I said.

I came there with him. He was my ride. How could he just leave and not even say anything? I was pissed. I asked someone to take me to his place. I was going to confront him. He couldn't just leave me at a party like that. When I got to his house, I just started going off.

"How the fuck are you going to just leave me like that!"

Before I got out another word, I saw stars. He hauled off and hit me right in the mouth. I was shocked, stunned. He didn't stop there. I had been staying with him at his aunt's place in East Orange and I had my things there. He went and got my stuff, balled up my clothes, and threw them out the front door.

Confused and angry, I ran onto the streets and started collecting my stuff. My mouth hurt and so did my pride. I was too through with him. I called a cab and went home.

The next day he came around talking about how he was sorry. Actually, he didn't say the words *I'm sorry,* but he started talking about his childhood and how nobody ever loved him and how he was feeling that I was playing him out by talking to other dudes at the party, and he just lost it.

I don't know why, but seeing him like that, all vulnerable and sad, I felt sorry for him. I could see this little boy who was abandoned, whom nobody loved, with all of this pain and anger, and I understood where he was coming from. He had me from that moment. I guess I could even excuse his hitting me. I had been hit before. And I was of the mind-set where I believed that if a man hit me, it meant he cared. For him to get that mad to have that much emotion, he must *really* care about me.

So our relationship sprang on that bungee cord. We had our ups when we were in heaven with each other, and we had our downs, when he would lose it and hit me. There were more ups than downs at this point, so I took it. I liked being with him more than I liked being without him. And when it was good, it was great. There was so much heat and passion between us.

We were together like that for eight years. On and off, back and forth, up and down. Then our relationship took another dip. Salt-N-Pepa was on the road touring. We were in Kansas and Brad flew in to surprise me.

Spin came running to me all excited. "Brad says he wants to get married!"

"Huh?"

"He wants to get married right now and I'm going to plan it."

What?! What kind of crazy proposal was that? He delivered the message through Spinderella. He flew out to Kansas where we were performing talking about "Let's get married."

I said, "Okay." And right there we started planning this wedding.

The day Brad proposed to me—or the day I found out he wanted to marry me—was exciting. I seemed to have been waiting all my life to get married. This was a little different from what I'd imagined, though, but we were definitely a different kind of couple.

It was my idea to get tattoos instead of rings. He was into tattoos and so was I, and I thought that it would be a cool way to seal our union. I thought if we got tattoos of our wedding rings, we could never take them off.

He got PEPA tattooed on his ring finger in a design that looked like a ring. And I got BRAD on mine. We decided to have the actual wedding in the tattoo parlor. With such short notice, it was the only place that agreed to have the ceremony, and it was actually perfect.

Everybody got into this "wedding." Spin wrote up the invitations. Now mind you, we're on the road in Kansas so everything was spur-of-the-moment and informal. I think the invitations were on a piece of regular paper and read something like *Come to Brad and Pepa's wedding,* and it had the place and time. Spin went around handing them out to the dancers, the engineers, the people in the hotel, and the other people working with us on tour.

All of the girls went out and bought matching outfits from the local mall. All of the dancers, and Cheryl, were my bridesmaids. I found an all-white outfit—a pair of white shorts and a white shirt. Brad had on all white, too.

Somebody decorated the tattoo parlor. They had a runner to make an aisle, and the stylist, Elena, hooked us up with these long feathers, and the bridesmaids lined up on either side of the aisle, holding the feathers over my head as I walked down the aisle. I even had a bouquet that we got from a local florist.

Spin was the minister. She did the whole "Dearly beloved, we are gathered here . . ." and the "I now pronounce you husband and wife . . ." thing. It was official and cute at the same time.

After the "ceremony," we had some champagne and people gave little speeches about how perfect we were for each other.

Somebody rented a limo and they made up signs: JUST MAR-RIED! We even had cans tied to the back and the whole nine. Somebody shot a video of it. It was so different and so us. The limo took us back to our hotel, where they had reserved the ballroom for our reception. We had a wedding cake and everything. It was nice. The only thing needed to make it perfect was to have my mom and family there. But my mom would not have been down for any foolishness like that. My mom would have been breaking on me. I knew if I was to have her blessing, I had to have a real wedding.

Brad was down to do that, too. But I was content with our Kansas "wedding." I didn't think that a piece of paper would make it any more real. We'd made it official. I *was* married and that was all that mattered. I could have lived with that because it was perfect. Maybe I should have.

But when we got home, as I expected, my mother was breaking on me for that sham of a marriage we had. It had made the papers and a few of the entertainment magazines and gossip rags.

"We don't do things like that," she said. "That is so low class! You should have a proper wedding."

A proper wedding? I always wanted a "real" wedding. I decided I would plan one. I would have my fairy-tale wedding. I would do it for my mother, and for me. But while I was focusing so much on the wedding, I didn't pay too much attention to the marriage and the relationship. The gown, the bridesmaids, the family, the party, the pomp and circumstance—I would have it all. The happily ever after . . . that was not in the picture.

CHAPTER FOURTEEN

Whatta Man

WE WERE PREPARING FOR THE video for "Whatta Man," which went on to be one of our runaway hits. The video featured these fantasy scenes where Cheryl, Dee Dee, and I got to make out with the man of our dreams. We sat around and made a list of the guys we wanted in the video. Cheryl and Dee Dee looked at me like "poor Sandy," because they knew I wouldn't have a choice.

"I guess Brad is going to be your fantasy man," Cheryl said, laughing. She knew he would never allow me to make out with anyone but him. She was right. Cheryl got to make out with Tupac Shakur, the lucky girl! We all loved him and he was so thuggish.

He almost didn't make the taping of the video because the

day before he had a shoot-out with the cops. He was in pretty bad shape. We taped around it. But we were adamant that he had to stay. Hurby was so image conscious that he was fighting us over that. He said he didn't want that kind of thug in our video. But we won that fight.

Tupac was cool. He was a good guy. I remember him telling me that he had never been in trouble with the law until he got into the music business—which he got into to have a better life. He had more drama around him as an artist than he ever had as a regular guy.

"Now ain't that some shit?" he said. "I ain't never had a record until I made a record."

It was a sexy video. And we were feeling ourselves. We had just come back from Russia, where we spent a couple of weeks on tour. It was a tough tour for us because we couldn't eat the food. The meat there was funny—even their McDonald's hamburgers tasted funny. So we basically ate nothing and worked out every day. We had a trainer with us on tour and had nothing really to do in Russia except work out and perform. When we came back, we were in the best shape of our lives—all of us.

It was a good thing, too, because before the tour we were the brunt of quite a few jokes. A few months before leaving for Russia, I went to see Adele Givens and a bunch of other comedians at the Theater at Madison Square Garden, which was called the Paramount back then. In her routine, she started talking about one of our songs, "Do You Want Me." She replaced our lyrics to talk about food. Then she said, "Salt-N-Pepa? More like Meat-N-Potatoes! Have you seen how fat those girls have gotten?" I sank down in my seat a little lower. I didn't want anyone to recognize me. I laughed to play it off, but I was saying, "Damn! We aren't that fat, are we?" Apparently we were. So going on that

Russian diet worked wonders for our careers. We came back looking like a million bucks and did the "Shoop" video, then followed that with one of my favorite videos, "Whatta Man." I just wish I could have had my dream sequence with someone else. I was thinking about Omar Epps. But Brad wasn't having it. He was right there in that video.

Once again, my career was going well. We had one smash hit after another. And once again, my private life was going in another direction altogether.

Brad and I were fighting, breaking up, making up, fighting, and starting all over again. This went on for years. The fights we had were crazy. I can't say that I never participated in them, but I certainly got the wrong end of them. One time we were getting ready to go out. I was ironing a pair of jeans and he started in on me about something. It was always something, and the arguments always started over nothing—figments of his imagination or some perceived thing that I had said or done. I sucked my teeth, which is just a Jamaican habit of mine. He stormed over to me and grabbed a handful of my extensions.

It always started with his pulling me by my hair. He would always go for the hair, I guess to get a good enough grip on me so he could smack me more easily. I wore a lot of microbraids back then. He would grab and pull on them so much that whole braids with plugs of my hair would come out. It's one of the reasons why I wear lace-front wigs today—the hair around my edges never grew back.

I had the hot iron in my hand and he had a handful of my hair. I lifted the iron, which was natural, and he said, "Bitch, you trying to burn me?!" And he went crazy. He grabbed the hand with the iron in it and was pushing the iron toward my face. I was struggling against him but he was too strong, and he ended up pressing that hot iron against my other arm. I heard my flesh sizzling and the smell was sickening. I started screaming from the pain. He dropped the iron and I turned to run, and when he went to grab me, his nail swiped across my eyeball and shredded my cornea. I ended up in the hospital with a third-degree burn on my arm from the iron and a torn cornea. My eye was really bad, it was dripping pus, and I had to wear an eye patch for a while.

The doctors called the police. They knew that my injuries didn't happen the way I said (an accident). They wanted me to press charges and the police were trying to get me to tell what really happened. But I wouldn't. When I got out of the hospital, I stayed with a friend.

Cheryl came over. She was so sad for me. "Come on, Sandy. You can't keep doing this."

I knew she was right. "Yeah, I'm through!"

I invited over a few of my girlfriends—Cheryl included—and had an "I'm Done with That Nigga!" party. I literally threw a party. I was done. A lot of people who knew what I had been going through were happy that I had come to my senses. They couldn't understand why I stayed. I couldn't understand it, either. We had champagne and toasted, "Bye-bye, nigga!"

I was so free that I started dating. After all, I wasn't really married and I was done with him, right? During my newfound single life, I met baseball great Gary Sheffield. A friend of mine had been trying to hook me up with this guy for the longest time.

"I have someone that you must meet," she said. "He would be perfect for you."

She never told me who he was. But I ended up bumping into Gary at a party, and we started talking. When my friend found out, she told me, "That's who I was talking about!"

Something was definitely there from the beginning. And things were going well until Gary started getting serious. I remember when I was going out with him, he started what I call interviewing me—asking me a bunch of questions. I know now he was feeling me out to see if I was the kind of woman he could settle down with, because he was looking to settle down. But all the time I was thinking, *This ain't going to work.*

He didn't want a woman that liked to party so much, and I *loved* to party. I was looking at him as if he was too slow for me. But I probably needed to slow my behind down a bit, and he was the perfect kind of guy for me to be with. I needed a man like that because I needed to change my ways and perspectives on relationships. I needed that kind of stability in my life, but I wasn't ready for it.

I went with him and a bunch of his friends to Jamaica after he won the World Series when he was with the Florida Marlins. He flew a bunch of us to the island on a private jet to celebrate. He booked a villa at the Half Moon where we stayed and partied for a whole week. It was the most fun I'd had in a while.

When I got back, here comes Brad. I was done. But he was sorry. I had a lot of male friends who were baffled by my staying with Brad. Sam Cassell, an NBA star, was one of my closest friends. He would say, "You ain't left that man yet? You ain't giving up Brad. Nobody is going to take you serious because you always going back and forth with Brad."

Sam knew me so well. He could see it even when I couldn't.

A few weeks passed, and sure enough, here Brad came with his sob story about how nobody loved him and how much he needed me. I know now I was listening to that because I had low self-worth. I put his needs before mine. I decided I needed to help him, that I could fix it and make it all better. I didn't appreciate the things that I needed to fix in myself.

I forgot all about me; I just wanted to fix his situation and make him happy. That's what women do. We become the banker, the mother, the sister, the friend. We become Mrs. Fix-It for everyone but us.

Being alone these last few years, I've had a lot of time to think about this, and I believe that losing my father and then losing my son's father had a big effect on me. I'd never felt pain like that from a man, leaving me empty. I was scared of being alone. I didn't want to be alone.

So I went back . . . again.

That's when I got pregnant with Egypt. Once I got pregnant, well, you know me. I had to make it work. I still had hope for that fairy-tale ending. I was happy when I found out I was pregnant. And I wanted a girl so bad. I just knew I was having a girl. I had a feeling. I was obsessed with wanting a girl. But I needed to know for sure, and I couldn't wait for her to be born.

Brad made me promise not to find out, not to get the ultrasound. And I promised that I wouldn't. But I couldn't help myself. I wanted to know. And when it was confirmed, it was my little secret that I carried around. I was smiling all of the time—yes, because I was pregnant, but also because I was carrying a little girl. And things were going well. To Brad's credit, in spite of the physical abuse behind closed doors, in public he was affectionate and he represented. There were never any disrespectful phone calls from women. When he performed and I was there, he would always acknowledge me; he even had a line where he talked about slapping "a heifer over Pep." We were a real couple.

When Egypt came, he was right there. He stayed in the hospital with me. He spent the night. He was there the whole time. We had a strange living arrangement. He didn't like staying in the mansion in Morris County. He liked being in his old hood in East Orange. He wanted me with him and asked me to move in with him. So I left my estate and moved into a small place with him in East Orange. Brad was a good father. He loved his little girl. He was good with Tyran, too.

He was there for all of the karate matches and the baseball games. If there was a family outing, he would be there. Even to this day, I will show up to a family function and Brad might be there with his girlfriend.

"I may have divorced Pep, but I didn't divorce her family," he says.

We had our family—the kids, Brad, and me—and I wanted to make it really official. My mother had been pressuring me about "living in sin." And she was embarrassed by our fake wedding in the tattoo parlor a few years before.

I loved the idea of being married. Always have. Brad and I had been together eight years before we had our fake marriage, and I was feeling that we might as well make it official.

So I set off to plan our "real" wedding. There were blood tests and paperwork. Tyran was the ring bearer, and Egypt was there, too, to see Mommy and Daddy tie the knot. She was really fussy and cried a lot. Perhaps I should have seen that as a sign. But I was too happy to let anything spoil this day.

We had flowers—beautiful, expensive flowers everywhere. The wedding was at my Morris County estate, a perfect location. In fact, I had a couple of weddings for others there. The place was better than any hall we could have rented. I pulled out all the stops. I spent about $185,000 on the wedding, including a $15,000 custom-made gown with real crystals and handmade beading. The train on my gown was ridiculous and beautiful. I still have that gown. Maybe Egypt will want to wear it one day. Shoot! Somebody had better wear it.

I practically built a cathedral outside, complete with hardwood floors, to hold the actual ceremony. I had acres on my estate, and the outdoor reception area was huge and elaborate. I turned my backyard into something out of a magazine.

About three hundred people were invited, including Vivica Fox, Foxy Brown, former New York Jet Curtis Martin, and of course Queen Latifah. Latifah and I had become close because Brad was her homeboy from East Orange, and that whole crew were tight—Kay Gee, Vinnie, Shakim (Compere, who is Latifah's manager and head of Flavor Unit), Brad, and La. Of course, she and I hit it off. She said Salt-N-Pepa were like her idols. We paved the way for her to do her thing, which was nice to know.

Latifah and Shakim gave us a honeymoon for our wedding gift that I will never forget. It was an all-expenses-paid, seven-day trip to the most beautiful resort I had ever seen, in Hawaii. There were black-sand beaches and everything was top-of-the-line. They didn't spare a single expense. It was amazing. Thanks, Sha and La!

The wedding was everything you could imagine. I didn't miss a single detail. We had everything, except for what was really important.

Brad never asked me to marry him—not really. He may say that he did, but he didn't. In Kansas, Spin came to me and told me he wanted to marry me. But he never got down on one knee and asked me to marry him. I never had that. Not with anyone.

Tah Tah at least gave me a ring. But that wasn't quite right either. Tah Tah gave me this box and then left the room. He didn't even wait for me to open it in front of him. He just said, "I hope it's okay," and left the room. He was worried about the ring's living up to my expectations. But I didn't have any expectations. All I cared about was the feeling behind the ring. The ring Tah Tah gave me apparently didn't have the feelings I wanted it to have. I didn't want a friendship ring, I wanted an engagement ring. I wanted to be married.

The best thing about being married to Brad was being able to say, "I'll have to consult with my *husband.*" If we had to have work done on the house or someone asked me about something, I could say, "I have to ask my husband about that."

I used to hear women talk about their "husband" and I liked the way that sounded rolling off the tongue. "My husband."

Brad was my husband.

It took us nine years of being together to finally tie the knot. Nine years of ups and downs. And by our tenth year it was all over.

I was reminded of how bad he could be one morning. I was scheduled to leave for an appearance in Jamaica in two days, so I was home resting. It was really early in the morning and he woke me to have sex. I wasn't in the mood and I kind of pushed him away gently.

"No, baby. Not now."

But he wasn't trying to hear that. He kept trying and I started pushing him away a little more forcefully. His behavior had been confusing me for a couple of weeks. He was distant and spending a lot of time in the streets with his boys.

So many good things were happening for me, for Salt-N-Pepa, and I was growing. He wasn't. His career was pretty much stagnant. I guess he was feeling something there. I don't know what was really going on inside his head. All I knew was that he wasn't listening to me this morning.

"No, Brad, I'm not feeling like it."

He kept grabbing.

"Stop!"

He stopped for just a second to look at me. He looked at me real crazy, as if he hated me. I had seen that look before and I was scared. I started pushing and crying. He had me twisted like a pretzel in some sort of wrestling hold, and I couldn't move. He was determined. He started taking it.

"Please, stop!" I said. "Okay. Okay. Let me fix myself."

I was in the most uncomfortable position. I couldn't move and my body was twisted. It was so painful. At the time I had an IUD, and I could feel it scraping against my insides, being shifted.

"Please let me fix myself," I pleaded with him.

He ignored me and got rougher and rougher. It felt as if he were killing me. I never believed that your man could rape you. But here I was getting raped by my man. He was worse than some stranger off the street. He was worse than my friend's grandfather. He was worse than my sister's boyfriend. He was worse than those guys who tried to gang-rape me when I was sixteen. He was worse because he knew me and he supposedly loved me and we had a life together and he never had to force it on me. I would always give it to him willingly and he knew it. I just didn't feel like it then. Maybe in another hour or two, he would have gotten it. But he took it!

After he took it, he didn't even look at me. He just got up and left. I lay there not believing what had just happened. I didn't want to believe it. When I tried to get up, I was in so much pain that I had to lie there for a few more hours. My whole body was just a ball of pain. I took a warm bath and tried to get myself prepared for my trip to Jamaica. I always loved going home, and this was going to be special because I had booked a couple of appearances. It was the one place where Pepa could be a star without Salt. They loved me there.

I didn't talk to Brad at all. He was staying clear of me and I really had nothing to say to him anyway. I was really looking forward to getting away.

I was at the airport, about to head to the gate at JFK in New York, when I collapsed. My knees buckled and I hit the ground and couldn't get up. I wanted to get up because I had made a scene and people were starting to gather around. But I couldn't move. They had to call an ambulance.

I spent seven days in the hospital. My entire body was infected, and the doctors said that I could've died. My IUD had ruptured my insides and bent my cervix. It caused a toxic reaction. I didn't tell the doctors that I was raped. They just simply treated it as a displaced IUD that caused an infection.

The doctors removed the IUD and told me I couldn't have sex for two months, which was fine with me. I was happy about that.

CHAPTER FIFTEEN

The Nightmare

I'M A FIGHTER. I WILL fight anyone. I have fought on behalf of my nieces, my sisters, even Cheryl. I will fight someone in the street who has something smart to say to me. But I would never fight in my relationships. I never fought back. I wasn't one to curse out any man I was with or put up resistance when he hit me. In my public life I am this loud, over-the-top, strong person.

In my relationships, I have been passive and obedient. I figured if I didn't fight back, maybe he wouldn't beat me so bad. And with Brad, I just knew if I didn't fight back, I could possibly end up at the bottom of a staircase, broken and dead—as I had seen in my dream.

I had been having this dream that I couldn't seem to shake. It was recurring and scary. Y'all know by now that I have visions, and when I see something, it always happens. But this was one vision that I was determined to never see come true.

In my dream, I was standing at the top of this huge staircase. This staircase was like something out of *Dynasty*—with its white, wooden railings that seemed to go on forever. It was the kind of staircase you find in a mansion, splitting two wings. The staircase was so huge that in this dream I couldn't stand in the middle and grab the railings—they seemed like a mile apart.

In my dream, I'm at the top of the stairs and I'm in a fight. I'm on the wrong end of this fight, with my back to this huge staircase. I'm being beaten and I'm not really fighting back because I'm over this staircase—this long, hard, wooden staircase—and if I fall, that's it. So I'm holding on to this person, trying to hold on to my life. But in my dream, I lose this struggle and end up at the bottom of this staircase broken. I don't know whether I'm dead or paralyzed, but I'm not moving.

I was barely speaking to Brad. I was recuperating from that last incident with the IUD. I spoke to him long enough to tell him about the no sex for two months. But why was I even entertaining being with him again after that? I was not in my right mind. I was not in a good place.

During this time, I got an invitation to hang out with a friend and her fiancé in California. Her fiancé was actor Omar Epps, and they had a beautiful house in the hills and a child together. Since I didn't get to go to Jamaica, once I was well enough to fly I decided to go chill with them. I had planned to stay a week and would leave the kids with my mom. It felt so good to be around friends. I told her everything that had happened, and she was happy to give me a place to get away from it all. We had so much fun those first few days catching up, laughing, sitting by the pool, playing cards, and talking. I couldn't drink because I was still on antibiotics, but I had just as much fun without drinking.

That fun, however, came to a halt when Brad showed up. He supposedly flew out to California after me to win me back. During the week I was there, Omar was telling me that I should give old boy another chance. And with his coming all the way to California, it showed that he really cared about me and our relationship.

"Just hear him out," Omar said. "You don't have to take him back, but he did come all this way."

I guess men stick together on things like this. I respected Omar. He made me a little open to hearing what Brad had to say, because this was my marriage and I was taught that you don't just bail out—no matter how bad it is. My parents stayed married, no matter what. That's what I was raised knowing. I didn't have a manual. And while I didn't like the way I was being treated, I couldn't really remember ever being in a relationship where it was good, where I was treated well. Maybe I thought this was normal.

Brad put his stuff in my room. He didn't really have much to say. It was weird, very weird. He was cordial, but still distant. He just flew in and was like "I'm here," acting as if nothing had happened, making small talk. As the evening wore on, I noticed he was drinking a lot. Everyone (but me) was drinking. But he was drinking a lot of hard liquor. And he kept drinking. Around one in the morning, I was ready to turn in. So I went to bed. He stayed up and drank some more.

When he did come up, he slid in the bed next to me and started feeling on me. I had to remind him about the two-month rule, doctor's orders. It had been less than a month since the incident.

"Can we just lie here and cuddle and just be here together?"
I said.

He seemed to be okay with it, and I fell asleep in his arms.
The next thing I knew, *tap, tap, tap*. I opened my eyes and he's
standing over me, looking at me with the same look he had
had in his eyes the morning he took it from me. I knew it was
trouble.

"Bitch, I want a divorce!" he said.

Oh, brother! I was looking at the door to see if I could make it
out. But he was standing in front of it, over the bed. This was it.
This was going to be his "one more time." I could see in his eyes
that he was going for it. He knew he was going to do something
and he didn't care. The last time he beat me, I told him, "I don't
care if it's five or ten years from now, you got only *one more time*
and I'm gone for good!"

I have this thing about me where I set dates. I set goals for
myself and stick by them. I may seem to be all over the place, but
I am really focused when I am set on doing something. When I
was smoking cigarettes for a small period in my life, I remember
setting a date when I was going to quit. I said that by December
28, I would not smoke another cigarette. I didn't cut back or
anything. I was smoking away right up through December 27,
and on December 28 that was it. No more.

So Brad had one more time. He might as well make it good
because this was the last time.

I sat up in the bed. "Okay," I said calmly, trying not to make
things escalate. But it was too late. He grabbed my ring, which I
had put on the nightstand before I went to bed, and threw it at
me with all his might. It was like a five-carat diamond and it hit
me right in the middle of my forehead. It was on!

It was about five thirty in the morning. The sun wasn't quite up. It was still dark out, but you could see the light squeezing through. I was dressed in this flimsy nightie—a camisole with matching silky shorts. I wasn't dressed to fight, and the door to the room seemed to be in another building. So I sat there and didn't react to his hitting me with the ring. I started to ease up in the bed, preparing myself for the next blow.

"Where're you going, bitch?!"

He grabbed me and yanked me out of the bed. It was a queen-size bed with a wrought-iron headboard and footboard. I thought it was pretty until Brad started slamming me into it. He picked me up by my throat, choking me, and he slammed me into the footboard. I felt as if my back had cracked open on the hard metal.

"Fuck you, bitch!" he said, grabbing me up again by my throat to throw me over the footboard. "You want out of this shit! You ain't trying to fix it."

He was choking me so hard, I thought I was going to black out. But I didn't. I started to get angry. Here I was catching a beating because I didn't really have much to say to him after he raped me. And then I couldn't have sex with him after the rape because he'd caused an infection that almost killed me. And he was beating me for that? Could I be mad for a little bit after all of that? Could I think for a minute before I just ran back and pretended everything was okay?

I always went back after a couple of days or a couple of weeks. This time, I might have needed a couple of months. I needed to make sure. I was going to take my time. I needed him to know I was serious and that he couldn't just do what he wanted anymore. Could I just take my time with this?

"Bitch, you ain't trying to work on this shit," he was now yelling, and throwing me into everything. I guess Omar and Kalima couldn't hear all of the noise because their bedroom was on the other side of this mansion. I was praying they would hear something and come and rescue me. My prayers were answered after he threw me into the glass credenza they had.

While they were making their way across from the other side, he banged my head into the wall several times and continued to choke me. I was scratching at his hands, trying to pull him off because I thought he would really choke me to death.

"Yeah, fight back, bitch! I want you to fight back!"

He was slapping me and choking me. Slapping me as hard as he could. It seemed to be going on forever. At one point, I had almost made it to the door, but he pulled me back by my hair and slammed me into the bed railing again. He was going crazy, as if he knew that this would be the last time he would have the chance to do this, so he was going for it. At one point, I looked up at him and gave him a smirk. I didn't say a word, but he knew what that smirk meant.

Get it all out now because I'm done!

I didn't know if I was going to make it out alive. But with each blow, I knew that this was it—I was *never* going back. This had to be one of the longest ass-whippings in history. But finally, the door swung open. Omar ran in and Kalima was right behind him, screaming and hollering for him to get off me.

Omar was trying to be real calm and cool. "Come on, man. Stop."

Kalima was calling Brad every name in the book and making him angrier. But he let go long enough for me to make a run for it. I hit the door and headed to the stairs. He ran after me, though, and caught me right at the top of the staircase. My back was to the stairs—these huge, *Dynasty* stairs. And he had a handful of my hair with one hand and was choking me with the other one. I was practically dangling over these stairs.

138

This was my dream, my nightmare, and I was living it out.

I knew how it ended in my dream, and I was bracing myself the best I could. There was nothing I could do. If I struggled and got him to let go, I was heading headfirst down these stairs with no way to break my fall. If I didn't struggle, he was certainly going to choke me to death.

"Man, let her go," Omar said in a calm voice. He had screamed moments before for Kalima to go to their room. She was making it worse, and he could see in Brad's eyes that he wanted to kill me.

"She's not worth it, man," Omar said. "She's not worth giving up your whole life. Let her go."

Brad released his grip and I turned around and hauled ass down the stairs. Out of my mind, I ran out the front door into the streets screaming, "He's trying to kill me! He's trying to kill me!"

I know I woke up the whole neighborhood—not that there were many neighbors. But a house two doors down opened its doors to me. I was beaten, bloody, half-naked, and scared for my life.

"Breathe," this lady kept saying. "Think of something that makes you happy. Think of a sunny beach and breathe."

She was some kind of therapist and was trying to get me to stop hyperventilating. I started to catch my breath. She was so nice. The police came to take my statement. The neighbors had called them. And while I knew I was never going back, I also wasn't strong enough to tell the truth. I couldn't press charges. I couldn't make him pay. So I lied.

Omar had taken Brad to a local hotel to get him away from me and the police. I didn't speak to him for a long time after that and I never went back.

That was his last time. That was it. I had to leave. I had to leave for my son, who was getting older and starting to understand some of the things that were going on. He wasn't really feeling Brad, and I knew it might get to the point where Brad would start putting his hands on him and I would have to go to jail for murder. I had to leave for my daughter. I didn't want her to think it was okay to live the way we were living, because it wasn't. But more than that, I had to leave for myself.

While I still didn't know for sure that I deserved better, I had an idea that I might. I knew for sure that I couldn't go back. Because I had said, "One more time and that's it."

And this was the one more time.

CHAPTER SIXTEEN

Beauty and the Beat

I HAD SPENT YEARS IN denial, running, hiding, and covering up for Brad. So many times I went places bruised and having to wear sunglasses or heavy makeup to cover it up. It was embarrassing. But for some reason, I rationalized it to myself. He was sick and I was the only one who could make him healthy.

What was worse, as I look back on it, was all the people who tried to help me move on—even people I didn't know well, such as Charles S. Dutton. He was the director on a movie, *First Time Felon,* that Brad and I did together. It also starred Omar Epps. It was really cool because this was my first real movie role, and I got to do it with Brad and one of my good friends, Omar.

Things were going well, but one night Brad and I argued over nothing in particular (and it was always nothing in particular), and he slapped me in my face. He was usually careful about hitting me in my face—especially if we had an appearance or something to do. He didn't punch me, but he slapped me so hard that my cheek was swollen. I had to go onto the set the next day with this red, swollen face. The makeup artist did her best to cover it up, but Charles Dutton noticed it.

He didn't really say much to me, but he invited me to stay in his apartment for the night while he stayed somewhere else. Charles told me it might be a good idea to clear my mind and be alone. He was so sweet. Charles sang this Reba McIntire song to me before he left for the evening. It was about this abused woman who kept making excuses for why her man kept beating her.

At first, I was denying that anything like that was going on. I was too embarrassed. But I just broke down and started crying. It hurt to wipe my tears over the bruise on my face. Charles Dutton was so understanding and wonderful. Opening up to him was one of the first steps I had taken to actually making a move. I wasn't getting beaten every day. But once was too much. It seemed that Brad was getting to a point where he didn't care. He didn't seem to care who knew.

After I came back from Charles's apartment, Brad could tell that something was different. I think he was even a little scared himself. And nothing ever seemed to scare him. He promised it would never happen again. He came back with the sob story and how he couldn't lose me. And like a dummy, I fell for it again. We got through the movie, and when it was over, we were back together.

There is a saying that love doesn't hurt. But that's the only thing I associated with love. As I said, I thought a man didn't love me unless he beat me or was rough with me.

My father was strict. He would beat any of us that got out of line. My sister Dawn caught most of the beatings. She was so rebellious, and my father would beat her so bad. I saw him beat her with an extension cord. I knew that my father loved Dawn. He loved all of us, even though he never said it. So it wasn't strange for me to think that a man could love me and beat me. My father split my lip after backhanding me once for sucking my teeth at him. It was one of the few times my father ever put his hand on me, and it hurt my feelings more than anything else because I was his favorite. But I knew that he loved me.

So when I heard a man say that he loved me, but he hit me, I believed that he loved me still. I never doubted it. In a sick way that showed me that he loved me more. He cared enough to get that mad.

I had developed this pattern. From the boy I gave my virginity to, to my first real boyfriend, Mike, to Ta-Ta to Brad and to all of the men in between, these men just weren't right for me, and I couldn't or wouldn't see it. That's what I thought I deserved. I was attracting these kinds of men because I wasn't right.

I'm not making any excuses, I just knew that I had to get right within myself. You can't have a good man unless you are okay inside yourself. I mean I had a few good men. There were Derrick Coleman and Gary Sheffield. But I wasn't really ready for them. You know what's wild? You can't really appreciate a good man when you're all messed up. You can't get a dime until you're complete in yourself—mind, body, and soul. Sometimes I think about how I was and what I accepted, and I can't believe that was me.

All of the drama and the chaos in my life around men started with me. It was what I accepted and what I expected. So I had to stop accepting it. That last time had to be the last time.

I know a lot of women are in relationships with men who hit them. And to them, maybe it's not so bad because he doesn't do it every day. And maybe he doesn't hit you, but he curses at you or talks down to you and makes you feel like crap. That's abuse, too.

Today, I can't take a man raising his voice to me, let alone putting his hands on me.

I tell a man straight-up before we get serious that I will not tolerate any of that. And if he even says the wrong thing, I'm out. No questions asked. No excuses. I understand that a person can slip and make a mistake. I would never tell a woman to leave a man the first time he hit her. Because people can bug out and make a mistake and never do it again. But if he does it a second time, then you *have* to go.

A man doesn't get a first chance with me. Not now. Not after everything I've been through. I'm gun-shy. I can't give him a chance. I love myself too much today to let that happen.

It took me a loooooong time to get there. But I'm there now. I am extreme like that. Brad knew it. He knew in his spirit that there was no sob story, no "I'm sorry," or anything else he could say. I was done. We had a daughter together and I definitely wasn't going to deny his being a father, but he couldn't have any access to me. My family and friends and everyone rallied around me and gave me so much love and strength and encouragement. They kept me up. But just the way that switch clicked over with Ta-Ta, that same feeling or lack of feeling clicked in now and I was really ready to move on.

I was grateful to have Salt-N-Pepa, my group and my girls, during this period in my life. We had our music. We had our fans. And all of our hard work had paid off too. We were considered among the greats. We even performed for Frank Sinatra to celebrate his fifty years in the business. Cheryl and I joked later about how he looked when we came out to perform "Whatta Man" for him. It looked like he leaned over to his wife and asked, "Who the hell are those girls?" But he played it off and Frank Sinatra seemed to enjoy it. Whether he knew who were or not, we were big enough to be asked to perform for Ol' Blue Eyes.

This was a big year for us because we were even nominated for a Grammy. It was the fourth time we were nominated, but this time, we actually had a chance. In the past, we were always up against Will Smith or Boyz II Men or somebody we knew we couldn't beat. Do you know how many Grammys we would have won if not for Will Smith?

We had won a couple of MTV Music Awards and were nominated for a Source Award. There was one year when we were at the Source Award praying that we wouldn't win. I remember Cheryl and I sitting there saying under our breath, "Please don't call our names! Please don't call our names!" We were nominated with Bone Thugs and Biggie and we just knew if they called Salt-N-Pepa that crowd would have exploded into boos. The Source Awards were very thuggish and very male dominated and we knew us winning wasn't going to go over well.

But we *wanted* to win this Grammy.

A Grammy meant that you had really done something. We were asked to perform on this night, which was also a good sign. You always see those groups perform and then their names get called while they are backstage and they cut to them screaming backstage.

Me, Cheryl, and Spin performed a medley of our greatest hits from "Shoop" to "Whatta Man" to "None of Your Business" (the last two songs we were nominated for). And we were still out of breath and sweating backstage when the presenters for our category took the stage. And when they announced the winners, *Salt-N-Pepa*, we weren't really paying attention. Somebody directed us to go out to the stage and we went out the wrong way. We looked like three blind mice. We ended up running across the whole stage to get our award. It was crazy and exciting. I don't even remember what I said. I was just excited and happy.

After we won, we ran into Oprah Winfrey backstage. I think she was a presenter. She congratulated us and told us how much of a fan she was, which was very cool. Then she invited us to participate in this race she was hosting the next day. It was some kind of race for fitness or something. This was the year when she was running marathons and all of that and she was pulling in as many women as possible to run this race with her. Of course, Cheryl and I said yes.

But we had just won the Grammy! I partied my ass off and didn't get back to the hotel until the sun came up. Well, Oprah had sent a car to pick us up for this race at six in the morning. When the phone rang, my head had literally just hitting the pillow. There was no way I was going running anywhere. I told my manager to make some excuse because I was in no condition to run in a race.

About ten minutes later my phone rang again.

"Oprah called herself and she said you had better be in that car!" our manager said.

Shit! I knew I had to drag my ass out of bed and I took a shower more to wake up more than anything and I got in that car. Cheryl was there, too, and she didn't look much more chipper than I was. It was six-something in the morning. Even when I'm not partying I don't get up that early!

It wasn't just that I hadn't had any sleep or that I might have had a slight hangover, but anyone who knows me knows that I'm not big on the physical exercise thing. And I never run. But there I was out there running in this race—me and Cheryl. We still laugh about that to this day because it was hilarious. The whole time we kept asking, "How much more do we have to run?" I was dying and it was hot as hell out there. I don't know if we made it even a mile.

But Oprah said we had better be there and there was no way we were going to disappoint Oprah Winfrey.

But a major transition was going on there, too. As I was getting rid of Brad, I was also getting rid of another man who had tormented me for so long—Hurby.

Cheryl and I were at the end of our contracts both for our albums and with our management. Cheryl, who was now in love with Gavin, had a child with him, and was completely moved on from Hurby. She was ready to move on from him in her career, too. What's funny is that by this point, I was cool with Hurby. We had an understanding, and now that my money was straight, so was our relationship. But Cheryl wanted him gone for good. So we paid him off. He put up a little bit of a fight, but those millions that he got were enough for him to just go away.

Cheryl and I were like two kids who had gotten out of school for the summer when we got rid of Hurby. She was particularly happy being in the studio without him. We wrote every song together, and she produced most of them herself. This album, called *Brand New,* was her baby. This was our liberation album. This was the real Salt-N-Pepa without the controlling Hurby telling us what to do. And we both knew it was going to be a huge success. After all, our last album, *Very Necessary,* had sold 4 million copies in the United States and another 3 million overseas. We had only had platinum successes in our entire career, so we expected *Brand New* to be even bigger coming off the huge *Very Necessary*. The anticipation alone would have people running to the stores to get it. Or so we thought.

I remember the interviews right before the album dropped. We did so many interviews. Cheryl was so into it all. She would tell everyone how tight we were.

"Our longevity is due to how close we are," Cheryl would say. "Pep is my sister!"

This was a moment for us. We had been together most of our adult lives, and now we were out on our own. It was a great feeling.

Then the album dropped. The reviews came first. None of them stood out, but I remember that most were lukewarm. The critics weren't really feeling this album. Then the audience gave their reviews. This was the first time we failed to hit the charts hard, and we barely sold gold, which was the worst feeling. We had never had that happen to us before.

Cheryl took it particularly hard. She took it personally because this was *her* album. She had put her heart into it. And for it to be rejected felt as if she were being rejected, and she couldn't handle it. She was depressed. Cheryl was hurt and nothing I could say would make her feel better.

I called it the Curse of Hurby.

"Girl, you know Hurby must have worked some voodoo on this one," I told her.

Cheryl got so mad when I said that. "He can't touch us with that!" she would say. "God wouldn't let nothing like that touch us. There's no such thing as voodoo!"

I'm Jamaican and I view that differently. I believe that curses do exist. Cheryl is spiritual and believes that God said nothing can touch us. But I know Jesus was casting demons out of people. I know that people were putting curses on people in the Bible, and while God can protect you, I know it can happen.

I think Hurby's father was into voodoo. I bugged out the first time I went to Hurby's house for a recording session. There were chickens and shit in the yard and in the house, and all kinds of symbols and voodoo stuff around the house. We used to joke about it all the time. But Cheryl didn't even want to entertain the thought. I'm not saying I know for sure that Hurby put a hex on us, but I wouldn't put it past him. The flop of that album just didn't make any sense. I believe that he felt that if we weren't going to be with him, we weren't going to be with anyone.

On the other hand, we were due for a flop. We had had so much success and so much of an easy ride in our career, we had to hit a valley. We had never even experienced bad reviews or poor-selling albums. Everyone has a bad spell. This was ours. I was willing to get back on the horse and ride it out. The only way to overthrow that bad run was for us to be strong together and work on another album and have a hit. We needed to be tight, to be a team, to be sisters. Cheryl wasn't strong. So it all went to hell.

CHAPTER SEVENTEEN

Joined at the Hip No More

I WAS SITTING IN THE pedicure chair at She Thing, Spinderella's day spa in Queens on Sunrise Highway. Salt-N-Pepa had done a magazine shoot the day before at the spa, and I decided to come back and get pampered. I was letting the massage chair work out the kinks while the pedicurist got the water the right temperature to start my pedicure.

As I was sitting there, my cell phone rang. I recognized the number immediately. It was Cheryl.

"Hey, girl!" I said.

"Pep, I just want to let you know that I don't want to be joined at your hip anymore!"

There was no hello. No "Hey, girl!" back. Just that. I was stunned.

"What?! What does that mean? What are you saying?"

"I can't do this anymore. I don't want to do this anymore."

"Oh. Oh, okay."

She was saying some other stuff. But I tuned her out. My heart started racing because I knew the tone, and I knew exactly what she was saying. But I didn't want to believe it. When she hung up, I just sat there.

Spin came over, I guess noticing the wild look on my face. "What's up?"

"That was Cheryl. She said she doesn't want to do this no more. She said she didn't want to be joined at my hip."

Spin was as stunned as I was. I mean, Cheryl had had moments in the past when she would go off or get all dramatic or act as if she was fed up. But this time seemed different. I hoped that it wasn't. But I knew that this time she meant it.

She said some other stuff that I couldn't really remember. It was all a blur. I know she mentioned regaining her life. She wanted her life back, she said. She said some things about the Lord and wanting to turn her life over to him and get out of the music business. But I kept hearing her talk about *her* life, getting *her* life back.

It was as if she had amnesia, as if all that we had accomplished was just hers to leave. In her mind, I guess, she was leaving me on good terms. We had just signed the biggest contract of our career. We signed for more money than we ever had. The deal might not ever have happened if I wasn't so persistent in getting out from Hurby's thumb. I was the one fighting for our independence. She thought that there would never be a Salt-N-Pepa without her. Well, there would never be a Salt-N-Pepa without me!

We were finally free. And it was Cheryl who'd wanted to

take it one step further. After I had negotiated for us to get more points. After I had brought in accountants to watch over the money, I was cool with everything—including Hurby. I just wanted us—Cheryl and me—to get our fair share. And now that we were, I was okay. It was Cheryl who wanted a clean break with everything—Hurby and management. It was Cheryl who was pursuing that.

"It will be just me and you, Pep," she said to me. "We can start over fresh with a clean slate."

We had finished our last album under our deal and were about to sign with a new label. Our contract with our management was up. The table was set for this clean slate. And I was excited to do it with Cheryl. I wanted to see what we could do together without Hurby and Carol, without the crutches. But when the album came out and it was a flop, the whole tone changed with Cheryl. She went from superexcited to superdepressed. She went from happy and optimistic to down and sad.

There was no contractual tie to Salt-N-Pepa anymore. So I guess Cheryl saw this as a perfect way out. We were doing interviews and promoting this album. And she knew she was planning on calling it quits. She knew all along she was leaving. I didn't.

I was making big moves, planning for my future. I had moved from Teaneck, New Jersey, where a lot of industry people lived. Biggie lived in my complex. So did Coco from SWV and Kedar Massenburg. There were also a couple of Giants football players and some professional basketball players. I left there and decided to look for a bigger house. My mom moved to Morris County with one of my sisters, and I wanted to be closer to them, yet close enough to the city.

I had a real estate agent that showed me a bunch of houses.

I had settled on one, but it didn't have a swimming pool and I wanted a swimming pool. He found me another with an indoor pool and enough acreage to build whatever I wanted. The house wasn't nice, but I knew what I would do with it once I got it. My mind started planning the bowling alley and the game room with the full-size video games, the pool table. I knew how I was going to trick out the indoor pool area. I could see it all. But I knew it would cost a whole lot, and I needed to be sure that I would have it like that. So before I put down the money, I called Cheryl.

"I want to buy this house," I told her. "Actually, it's an estate. But I'm nervous. I mean, it's so much money."

"Girl, you're going to be making a lot of money," she said. "This album is going to do well, and you'll have more than enough. Girl, do it!"

Cheryl was encouraging me (as she always did). But while I was running headlong into major debt, she was mapping out her exit strategy. Maybe she didn't know for sure that she was leaving. But she knew that I was building for the long haul, and I don't think she took any of that into consideration. When she wanted out, she just left.

And on her way out, she tried to make me feel as if it were all my fault. She said I resented her. She told me that she was the one who'd kept the group together all these years.

"And I'm tired!" she told me.

She told me that I never acknowledged all the things she did. She told me that they (she and Hurby) had had to carry me, that I was late all the time (which was true, but I never missed a date or a flight). It was easy for them to be on time. The studio was in Hurby's home and they could just roll out of bed and into the studio together.

She didn't remember or consider that I was the one that got us more money and changed the deal. I was the one out there hustling to get us other things outside the music.

When I got pregnant, Hurby took my money and paid Dee Dee more. But when Cheryl got pregnant, she didn't get a pay cut. She knew that was going on and she said nothing. She didn't consider all the things I had had to put up with and keep quiet about. And for the most part, I did keep quiet because I saw the bigger picture. I didn't want to cut off my nose to spite my face. But did I have an opinion about everything? Of course I did. I just wasn't willing to potentially ruin all we had built to get my point across.

I knew and I know that it wasn't all Cheryl and Hurby. I played a part in our success. I know I added something to the group.

When Whitney Houston called and wanted us to do a version of "Shoop" for her, I didn't say a word when management had Cheryl write the song for Whitney. Whitney was a huge fan of ours and she loved "Shoop" and wanted a song for the sound track to *Waiting to Exhale*. "Shoop" was my song. I wrote our "Shoop," that was my concept. I had to fight for Hurby to put the song on the album and I had to convince Cheryl to do it. It ended up being one of our biggest hits. But that song was mine and they had Cheryl do it. I prayed to God that Whitney would reject her song. Had she recorded Cheryl's version of my song, I would have been so hurt. So I was happy when Whitney didn't want Cheryl's version and had someone else do her "Shoop Shoop."

But Cheryl never said, "No, that's Sandy's song, she should do it." And I didn't want to make waves, so I let it slide.

When we were first starting and we had our first BS deal, I looked at the papers, saying, "This ain't right. I don't want to sign." I told Cheryl. But she signed.

"You want to be Pepa or not?" Hurby said, bullying me.

I didn't want to sign. I knew it wasn't a good deal for me and Cheryl. And I wasn't going to sign. But I did because Cheryl took away our power. Had she held out, too, they would have had to negotiate and come up with a better deal. But she didn't fight then. She was quiet. She could have said something. She had more power than I did.

I was there for her through all her drama with Hurby. I was a friend through all of that. And it was bad. On our first road trip, we drove in Hurby's VW Beetle; it was orange and he called it the LuvBug. It was snowing and he made Cheryl get out and pump gas in the snow. He was so mean and disrespectful. He thought he could get away with anything—and he could. He was having his cake and eating it, too. And the more success we had, the nastier and more arrogant he became. But I was there for her.

Hurby and I started off as friends. But by the end, I wanted to hurt him. One time, I told Cheryl that I was going to get some-one to whip his ass. I meant it, and Cheryl knew that I meant it, and she knew that I knew people who would be more than happy to whip Hurby's ass. I wanted him hurt for what he was doing to her and to us.

"Sandy, please don't," she said. "That's still my man. I know how you feel, but please don't. For me."

I didn't want Hurby killed, but if he ended up in the hospital with a few broken ribs, I would have felt a lot better about everything. That's how messed up he was and that's how mad he got me.

He was so disrespectful to Cheryl that he would just do things—such as have chicks on the side everywhere—and didn't care who saw him. (He was really into Asian chicks. Hurby was rolling with Asian girls before it became popular.) If anyone in our camp tried to pull Cheryl's coat, he would fire them. I would ask her, "Why would you do this?" I would get her thinking that she didn't have to be treated like that. I was there always with some fun to be had, someone to hang out with, a new man to introduce her to. Every boyfriend she ever had outside of Hurby, I introduced her to him.

She said she was my therapist, and she was. I had a lot of shit to get through. But I was her therapist, too.

We were there for each other. As much as I would trip from time to time, I also had Cheryl's back. I was there ready to do battle when T knocked her out. While Hurby was running away, I was there.

She was small but she was feisty. She wouldn't back down from an argument. As many fans as we had, there would also be some haters out there starting stuff with us. I walked up on a girl in Cheryl's face after an appearance early in our career. Cheryl was right there with it, yelling in the girl's face. The girl was threatening to take off her shoes and beat Cheryl up. Now this girl was my size, and while Cheryl could have held her own, I'm sure, I wasn't going to let her fight this girl. So I jumped in.

We had bodyguards who were prepared to step in and stop it. But I told them not to. I was going to handle this. I was never known to stand there and actually fight and scratch and all of that. There were too many chances to get your face scratched up or get punched or something, and I wasn't having that.

I was known for grabbing, dropping, and choking people. I learned that move from Dawn. If you get people down and apply some pressure to their trachea, they will definitely stop fighting you. Cheryl used to joke that I would catch a case one day and mess around and kill somebody. Thank God, I never did.

This girl was all ready to fight the old-fashioned way. "Bitch, what you gonna do?" This girl was real tough.

I didn't say a word. I just grabbed her and got her down on the ground and applied the choke hold. I felt her grip loosening, so I knew she must have been getting light-headed. Somebody called the cops, so I let the girl go, and Cheryl and I jumped into the limo and sped off.

I had her back because we were in this together. We were a team. We were joined at the hip because that's what worked. We went together like salt and pepper.

Cheryl said she wanted to leave because she couldn't breathe. She couldn't handle it anymore. What I think Cheryl couldn't handle was the disappointment of the music not doing well. She couldn't handle failure.

But even though that CD didn't do well, I didn't think we were through. Everyone has those bumps in the road. We weren't finished because this album went gold instead of platinum.

And maybe I could have accepted what she said if I thought she was telling me the truth. Cheryl said she wanted to give her life over to God. Who could argue with that? She said she was walking away from the business to serve the Lord. I could handle that.

But then she signed a deal with Virgin Records and she's calling herself the Salt of the Earth. When Beyoncé went solo, she didn't call herself Destiny. Because that's associated with her group. When SWV broke up, Coco was just Coco. She didn't call herself S or W or V. You leave a group, you can't hold on to that name. That was one thing that really bothered me. She could not be Salt without me. She needed to just call herself Cheryl if she was going to do the solo thing.

But what really bothered me was when I heard cuts from

the album. It didn't sound like gospel to me. It sounded like the same stuff we were doing as Salt-N-Pepa, and her leaving felt more personal against me than something she was doing for herself, and that I just couldn't take. Because it was all a lie.

She said she couldn't create and make the music she wanted being with me. But *Brand New* was all her creative energy. I let her do whatever she wanted. I never made it that serious. I got mad, sure, from time to time about her trying to control too much. But eventually, I would back down. And she knew I would always back down.

So she left me for dead. She saw her chance and she took it. She had it all planned out. The day Cheryl called me in Spin's salon, she talked about regaining her life.

While she gained a life, I lost mine. . . .

When I got home from the spa, I went to the bathroom and locked the door behind me. I took a disposable razor from my medicine cabinet and started making little slices along my wrist. I wasn't trying to kill myself. I was trying to get rid of the pain.

The first time I cut myself was after my father died. Making those little cuts right on the surface hurt so much at first, but after I made about three or four slices, the pain started to feel good. It actually made the pain in my heart feel less. I have no idea where I got this idea. The first time I did it, I used one of my father's razor blades. He had an old shaver. It was metal and you had to twist the bottom to open it up to replace the double-sided razor blade. I think I wanted to feel close to him. Please don't ask me to explain what kind of sick thought was going on in my head, but I know I wanted to use his razor and somehow I got around to cutting myself with it. Maybe back then I did really want to kill myself. But I never sliced deep enough and I learned later that if I wanted to kill myself, I had to cut against the artery the long way.

A lot of people looked at me as the strong one of the group. I was the tough one. I was only tough for someone else. I would fight for anyone. I would be tough to protect my family or friends. I never showed weakness around other people. I was weak around myself. I never fought for me. Not even when Cheryl left. I just let her go.

I don't want to be joined at your hip anymore!

What did that mean? We had been Salt-N-Pepa for most of our adult lives. We had been successful. We became famous together. We became rich together. We were right in the middle of our success, we were at the heights, and she just wanted to end it and I had no control. *What could I do?*

I made another slice to try to kill the pain.

What would I do now? I didn't know how to do anything else. Being Pepa was who I was. And I wasn't Pepa without Salt. So was I nobody now?

I made another slice.

I went from cutting myself to destroying my life. I went buck wild partying. I was always partying, but I took it to another level. I was out every night. And I was spending money like there was no tomorrow. I went out and found me another man and married him. And he ended up costing me millions. I'm in court to this day to try to get some of that money back. He bought a bunch of property in my name. He had credit cards on my account and everything. I ended getting rid of everything that reminded me of that time—including my home.

CHAPTER EIGHTEEN

My Surreal Life

CHERYL HAD LEFT ME FOR dead. I had this man—my second husband (no, I'm not going to talk about him because I'm still in court dealing with his mess)—trying to spend up all my money and put me in the poorhouse. I set up a good friend of mine to have her own business, and that, too, ended badly with her borrowing a bunch of money and not paying me back. I was Pepa, from Salt-N-Pepa, and no one wanted to book just me to do anything.

I got asked to do a few appearances and a bit part in a couple of movies, but nothing close to what I was used to. Nothing close to what I wanted. I wanted to perform onstage. I wanted to do music—my music. I wanted to be back on top.

I got a call from my publicist at the time asking me if I wanted to go on this new reality show on VH-1, called *The Sur-*

real Life. After a couple of seasons it seemed to be pretty popular. At this time MTV and VH-1 were the only networks really popping the reality shows, and of course there were the shows like *Survivor.* But the *real* reality shows hadn't taken off yet. There wasn't a *Flavor of Love* or an *I Love New York.* There wasn't a *Wife Swap* or a *Biggest Loser.*

I don't watch television, so I didn't know about any of these shows, anyway. I had never seen an episode of *The Surreal Life.* The only things that I watched were soap operas—*The Young and the Restless* and *The Bold and the Beautiful.* And I taped those and didn't usually get around to watching them for two weeks—you could not watch a soap opera for years and be able to pick right back up with it. So I had no idea what *The Surreal Life* was.

They told me the concept and I thought it would be cool. I'm an entertainer by nature. I love to entertain and I missed being in the spotlight. All I had to do was live in a house with a bunch of people and be myself and they would pay me? That sounded great.

A couple of my friends were telling me I should think about it. Omar, whose career was going well with *Love and Basketball,* and a hit TV show, *House,* was telling me, "I don't know if that's a good look for you and your career. I think you're too big for a show like that. I mean, it's a reality show."

He was thinking that a reality show would ruin any chances I might have at actually having an acting career, which I was dabbling in. I thought about it. And with no touring and no recordings and no nothing, I figured, what did I have to lose? I might have been taking a chance. But at least I was making some money and getting my name and face back out there.

We had a crazy cast. There was Bronson Pinchot, the guy who played Balki on *Perfect Strangers,* baseball great Jose Canseco (who set off the whole steroids thing), motocross racer Carey

Hart, supermodel Caprice, former supermodel Janice Dickinson, and Omarosa from *The Apprentice*.

Oh my goodness, Janice and Omarosa were off the hook with their fights.

A lot of people thought that the whole thing was an act just for the cameras, but those fights were real. And they were petty. Omarosa and Janice were roommates, which I'm sure the producers thought would bring fire, and it did.

Omarosa had unpacked her things and had her shoes and clothes neatly on her bed, and when she came back in, she found her shoes thrown in the corner on the floor. She got ready to go to sleep one night and found her bed had no sheets or pillows. She suspected that Janice had taken them off. And then the insults started back and forth, and some of the stuff was crazy.

"Your mama!" Omarosa would yell after Janet called her a no-talent bitch or something.

Janet would yell back, "No, *your* mama!"

It was really crazy. And I ended up in the middle, as each person came to me complaining about the other. I was the only one in the house who would listen. Everybody hated Janice because she was just too much. But I understood her.

I didn't have any problems with Janice. She was older than everyone else and kind of set in her ways, and she had some issues. Hell, she told us she had issues as soon as she came into the house. My thing was, if this woman is telling you she has issues, why antagonize and agitate her? I think Omarosa may have been pushing Janice's buttons in the beginning for the drama for TV. She was a veteran of the reality-show stuff because of *The Apprentice* and had done a couple of other reality-type things. She knew what would pop for her on camera, and setting Janice off would definitely bring the fire. But then it got serious because Janice wasn't playing with her.

I think Omarosa crossed the line when she called Janice a crackhead on camera. Now I saw Janice drink—we were all drinking at some point. I mean the liquor was flowing freely in that house. But no one saw Janice using drugs. And when Omarosa did that, it really set Janice off because she has kids and didn't want them thinking that what Omarosa was saying was true.

The crazy thing was that Omarosa went behind the scenes and apologized to Janice, saying that she didn't mean for it to come off like that. And when Janice made that an issue and tried to get Omarosa to apologize on camera, Omarosa acted as if she'd never apologized and had no idea what Janice was talking about. That's when I thought, *Oh, that girl is working this.* And I didn't think it was cool. Because you're talking about people's lives. This was a show, but in the real world we all had lives to go back to, and having people say certain things could hurt your real career.

I thought Omarosa should have apologized for that on camera. Janice was work, but as I said, I had no problems with her. I chalked it up to Janice being Janice. I just felt that most of the cast was judgmental. People have issues. I know I do, and I wasn't willing to judge her for her issues.

I really it hit off with Caprice. She's the only one that I stay in touch with to this day. It was just instant. She was wild and crazy, like me. She is so European. And she loved adventure. We were roommates, along with Jose Canseco. But he never stayed in the room. He stayed on the living room couch for most of the show. So Caprice and I really got to know one another.

It did feel like a family for those weeks. After the first couple of days you kind of forget that there are cameras everywhere. In the beginning I was careful about what I would say and do. I definitely stayed away from the Jacuzzi because I knew there would be trouble. There was too much alcohol and too many crazy people for me to end up in the Jacuzzi with them. I could just see the pictures online. And I'm never really sure what I might do. I know me, and sometimes I might do just about anything.

That's what happened with the banana incident. Once again I got caught up in a dare. That's my thing. Please don't dare me, because I am likely to do it. So when the dare came up about the banana, I took it. I had done similar tricks on the road with Cheryl and Spin with a cucumber, so I knew I could put the whole banana down my throat. The cucumber I used was much bigger. I know a lot of people had nasty thoughts when I did that.

It ended up being a hit on YouTube, too. They had so many versions of it, including one that was done in fast motion. People had it as their screen saver. I had fans coming up to me on the streets wanting to talk about that banana trick. I've had a couple women tell me that their boyfriend or husband wanted them to try it. I even heard somewhere that a few people choked to death on a whole banana. I pray to God they didn't die trying my trick.

And that's just what it was, a trick. I had practiced it many times before, using first a carrot, then a cucumber. It was a trick like those of magicians that stick fire and swords down their throat. It's the same thing. And I have that trick mastered. So please, do not try it at home.

After I got home I got so much flack for it. The only regret I have in doing it was for my son. I didn't want him to catch any teasing from his friends because his mother can put a whole banana down her throat. Other than that, I was proud of it. But please don't ask me to do that trick today because I haven't practiced it in a while.

It was surprising to a lot of my friends that that was the only crazy thing they caught me doing on camera. People would ask me why I was so quiet. People would always come up to me and say, "You're so crazy, why were you so quiet on *The Surreal Life*?"

Because I am so crazy I had to make sure that nothing came out of my mouth that I would regret. There was so much liquor and so much drama and chaos that it would have been easy for me to get caught up in some shit.

I only thank God that there were no fine brothers on the show. The only cute guy was Carey Hart, and he was married to Pink at the time, so he was very off-limits to me. Jose was cute, too. But he wasn't paying anyone any attention.

Come to think of it, why don't they ever have any fine brothers on those shows? Think about it. We get Emmanuel Lewis (no disrespect, Manny, because you know I think you are a sweetheart and a beautiful man), Gary Coleman, George Jefferson (Sherman Hemsley), and Flavor Flav! You have got to be kidding. So without a love interest, I had no problems on *The Surreal Life.*

My only scary moment wasn't on that season, but the next. After *The Surreal Life,* I was invited back for something called the *Fame Games,* which brought together some of us from previous seasons of *The Surreal Life* to compete against one another in a bunch of different events to prove who had real fame.

Robin Leach hosted it, and there were me, Rob Van Winkle (Vanilla Ice), Ron Jeremy (The Hedgehog), Verne Troyer (Mini Me), Brigitte Nielsen, Emmanuel Lewis (*Webster*), C. C. Deville (rocker), Andrea Lowell (*Playboy* playmate), and Traci Bingham (*Baywatch* babe). Manny was really cool. What a nice, sweet man. He used to get up every morning and cook us breakfast. And he had a way about him. I can see him making someone a nice husband.

Ron Jeremy and I used to get into these deep discussions. One time, we were talking about religion. I should have known better. Ron is Jewish and I was telling him that the only difference between Jews and Christians is that they believe that Jesus was just a prophet and we Christians believe he was the Messiah. I was trying to prove to him why the Jews missed the boat on Jesus, and if Jesus was such a great prophet, what prevents him from being the Messiah? It seemed like a friendly enough conversation. But Rob came over and whispered in my ear, "Be careful."

I didn't understand what he meant. He pulled me aside and said, "Be careful talking about Jewish people. You don't want to get caught out there. Just be careful. Like you're calling them Jews, they are *Jewish*. Calling them Jews is offensive. Just be careful. You know that they can cut up the tape any way they want, and they can make you look crazy. Just shut up!"

I got scared. And I started thinking about what I had said and if it might be taken as offensive. I ended my conversation with Ron Jeremy and headed for the room with the special phone that went directly to the producers, and I told them that I wanted that whole conversation cut out of the show.

They told me not to worry, that it wasn't bad. But I wasn't taking any chances. Here I was trying to reclaim my career; I didn't need some misunderstanding to stop me before I got started again. My grandmother is Jewish and I'm not prejudiced at all, but you never know how things can be taken. I was nervous about it.

It ended up being all right. But I was on pins and needles until that episode aired.

I should have won the *Fame Games*. And I would have won but I kept second-guessing myself. It was a great experience. The money was good, too. They paid you a certain amount just to appear on the show. And for every day you stayed in the game, you got another $5,000. Not a bad day's work, huh? You're there for a month and they feed you, you have nice accommodations, and you never have to come out of your pocket for a thing. It was a like a monthlong, all-expenses-paid vacation that they pay you to go on. And I got to hang out with some interesting people.

People knock reality shows, but some people make a living doing them. That's what Omarosa is doing, and I'm not mad at that. It's better than working in an office, that's for sure.

One of the best things that came out of doing *The Surreal Life* was my friendship with Caprice. She was like a European version of me—just as wild and crazy. We keep in touch, and either I go to Europe or she comes here, but we try to hang out at least once a year. In 2006, Caprice invited me to do the Gumball Rally with her. This was a seven-day, thirteen-country, three-thousand-mile auto race through Europe. It was one of the craziest things I had ever done (which is saying a lot). The race was not just on highways with regular speed limits where you would have to break the law if you wanted to win; it was also on regular roads and residential streets. There were no rules. In 2007, two people were killed in this race. I had planned on being there for that one, too, but I had business in the States.

Y'all know it's hard for me to stay away from a thrill. So when Caprice called me to be her partner in the Gumball Rally, I was all in. Caprice knew about my adventures and my racing skills from our talks when we were roommates on *The Surreal Life*. Caprice knew about the times in Queens when I nearly got arrested or killed for doing something crazy on the road, usually with Cheryl riding shotgun.

Cheryl and I were like Thelma and Louise back in the day on the roads. Most of the crazy things I've done in a car, Cheryl was right there in the passenger seat. Such as the time I got busted backing up on an on-ramp of the Grand Central Parkway. I used to get on at the wrong place all of the time and realize it and back up on the highway and off the on-ramp. One time, the cops were sitting at the top of the ramp waiting for me. I turned to Cheryl and said, "You know what I'm about to do, so don't laugh."

I had gotten pulled over quite a few times for speeding and doing other illegal things. But I planned ahead. I figured I would eventually get caught, and I had better have a good story ready. So I had different stories prepared for different occasions. If I was caught speeding, I would wet my face, and as soon as I rolled down my window, I went into hysterics, crying and screaming. I would tell the cops that someone was chasing me and that I was scared and didn't know what to do. I would just be out of my mind and shaking. They always believed me, and they would start taking my statement, asking me what color car it was and a description of the driver. They would ask Cheryl or Sonya, or whoever was in the car with me, to confirm my story, and they had better back me up.

People who rode with me knew that somehow I was going to make it out. My sixth sense definitely came in handy on the road. I seemed to know where the danger was before I got to it. I have never had an accident, and I have never gotten so much as a ticket—not once. One time, they even gave me a police escort to the hospital. I would keep ketchup in the car and put it up to my mouth with a tissue and act as if I were coughing up blood. Look, I would do anything, because with the kinds of illegal stuff I was doing, the kinds of speeds I was driving, they wouldn't have just given me a ticket, they would have thrown my behind in jail.

So Caprice knew about all of that when she asked me to roll with her in the Gumball Rally. She knew I would be her perfect road dog. I told my mother I was going to Europe to hang out with Caprice. I had her watch my kids and I was off.

Maximillion, the guy who started the Gumball Rally, gave us a black Porsche and a waiver on the $30,000 entrance fee. I met

Caprice at the starting location in London, England. Before I left, Caprice told me to pack light. I packed as light as I could . . . for me. She knows me well, so when I showed up with these two huge bags, she rolled her eyes. There was hardly enough room in the back for my bags. They were so big that we couldn't see out of the rearview mirror. It was so funny. I had to tell her if something was coming up by looking at the side-view mirror. Caprice was pissed.

We spent the first part of the trip arguing. Actually, she was arguing with me.

"Keep both hands on the wheel!" she would say.

"You're going too fast!"

"Pay attention to the road!"

I would be talking while I was driving and looking at her while I was talking, and it was driving her crazy because we were going like 180 miles an hour with traffic on the roads. But I'm used to that. And I would have one hand on the wheel, and the other hand would be gesturing while I was talking. Caprice was serious. She kept both hands on the wheel and eyes on the road.

While we knew we probably wouldn't win this thing because quite a few professional drivers were in it, we didn't want to be the "girls" of the bunch. We were the only all-girl team, but we were *not* coming in last. A few of the guys brought a lady with them, but the women were more window dressing than drivers. This was a grueling race. You had to know how to drive to be in it.

We would leave early in the morning from a city and drive for seven hours until we got to the next destination. There, we would party until the wee hours, get maybe two hours of sleep, and be back on the road the next morning. You really needed two good drivers to do this for seven days straight.

And I *had* to go to every party. When was I going to have a chance to party in Prague, Berlin, Vienna? And everything was top-of-the-line. The best hotels, the best liquor, the hottest music. It was crazy. By the third day, Caprice finally calmed down with my driving and started feeling herself, too. Whenever one of the guys pulled up next to us, she would send it into overdrive. She wouldn't let anyone pass us.

I even got up to two hundred miles an hour a couple of times myself. We never got caught, though. A few people got pulled over for speeding. One car had a police helicopter swoop down on it. So the speeds we were doing were not legal in most countries. Only in Germany could we really open it up.

That was the fastest and the most tired I had ever been while driving—mostly because I didn't get any sleep. Caprice would fall out when it was my turn to drive. While Caprice is one of the few people I would ever allow to drive like that with me in the passenger seat, I still wasn't going to shut my eyes on her going that fast. Uh-uh, I could not sleep while Caprice was driving. So I was lucky to get a couple of hours after partying.

We were ripping through the beautiful countrysides of England, Austria, and the Czech Republic. Some of it I couldn't take in because we were moving so fast, but it was quite an experience. I had heard about the autobahn and was excited to be driving on it. It was like a huge raceway with no limits. It was raining though when I got there and the road was slick and I'm not stupid, so I kept it reasonable. I couldn't get busy the way I wanted to. But that didn't stop some of the nuts we were with, who were spinning out and getting into accidents. You have to know what you're doing out there. You have to know how to handle those conditions. I am careful enough to slow down under those conditions.

As we head into the final stretch of the race, the last two days, I'm completely wired. I'm on everything from Red Bull to Vivarin to No-Doz. I am so amped on caffeine that even if I tried to sleep, I couldn't. Thank God neither Caprice nor I did drugs, or we might have been finished for sure. We were representing for the ladies and I was proud of us. I was looking forward to the final party, which would be on a yacht in Monaco, where we would party for the entire weekend.

It was the Thursday before the final destination and Caprice and I are doing our thing on the road. She was driving and all of a sudden I got this crazy vision.

In my mind I could see a whole scene play out, like a movie. I have had these visions since I was young, and it has taken me most of my life to be okay with them. Sometimes I can see sickness, and if someone needs to get something checked out, I can tell him or her. Sometimes I've seen dead people, spirits who want to deliver messages to loved ones, and other times I have seen death. This was a death vision and I was part of it.

In my vision, I saw the left, back tire of the black Porsche we were driving blow out. I saw Caprice driving. She lost control of the car and spun out right near the side of a cliff. We went over the cliff, which was hundreds of feet in the air. And we died. I saw her mother at her funeral crying.

After the vision, I sat quietly in the car—our black Porsche. Caprice was driving. I thought about whether I should tell her. I knew for sure that I had to get out of this car. My visions *always* come true. Sometimes it may take a couple of days, or it may be a couple of hours. I have no way of knowing. All I knew was that I didn't want to see this vision come true.

"Pull this car over!" I finally started to scream. "Pull over! Pull over!"

"What? What's the matter?!" Caprice was alarmed but she wasn't pulling over. She was racing next to a car that was in the race—two cute guys were in the next car and Caprice wanted to show off. But the faster she went, the crazier I became.

"Yo, slow this shit down, now! I had a vision and we die!"

At first she laughed. "Oh, Pep, come on!"

Then she looked at me and saw I was dead serious. Caprice had seen these visions in action when we were on *The Surreal Life* together. She knew I had these powers, and she knew I was serious. She slowed down and I told her what I saw.

"We only have one more day after this one," she tried to reason with me. "Don't you think if we take it easy and are careful we can make it to Monaco?"

She really wanted to go to that party. Hell, so did I. But according to my vision, we weren't going to make it anywhere if we stayed in this race. She pulled into the next stop to get some petrol, as they called it in Europe. And I was hysterical.

"I'm not getting back in that car!" I screamed. "Don't you understand? We die! I saw it, Caprice. We die!"

I was yelling and screaming about taking a plane home from there, and some of the other teams had pulled in to get gas and were looking at me as if I were crazy—this crazy black woman, looking like something off *Jerry Springer,* ranting and raving in the middle of Europe about a vision of dying. I didn't want to spoil the trip for Caprice. But I was panicking at the thought of getting back in that car.

"I'm not driving, yo!" I told her. "I'm not getting back into that car."

I started to hitchhike. I saw a truck pulling up for gas and I tried to ask the guy if he could take me to the next big city where I could catch a plane. But of course he didn't speak English and I definitely didn't speak whatever he was speaking.

Caprice came over to try to calm me down. "Pep, come on. Let's just drive to the next stop and talk about it then. I promise to take it easy. I will take it down to eighty or a hundred miles an hour."

"Eighty or a hundred?!" I screamed. "When I say slow down, I'm thinking fifty. When is a hundred miles an hour slow?"

Considering we were pushing two hundred, I understood why she thought eighty to a hundred was slow. But it wasn't slow enough to save our lives. I knew that.

Some of the guys started coming around telling me how I was overreacting.

"We have one more night," they said. "You can make it to Monaco. Stop worrying. It will be okay."

But they didn't understand. I *saw* it. And what I see *always* happens. Caprice believed me, but she just thought that if we took it easy, we could make it.

"Come on, Pep. Let's just try," she said.

My heart was torn. I didn't want to mess this trip up. But I also knew that I shouldn't be going against my grain like this. We looked into getting a new tire for that back, left wheel, but they were special tires and this petrol station didn't have any. I tried everything but finally I decided to go.

I got in the car, my asshole shaking, and we drove to the next stop. We didn't party when we got there; we fought the whole night because we had one more day until the end and Caprice wanted to finish and I wanted to go home. The next day, it still wasn't settled. The other teams had left around seven in the morning and it was now nine, and Caprice and I were still at the hotel arguing. I finally decided, against my better judgment, to go with her. She said she was leaving without me, and I couldn't let her get in that car and drive alone. I was trying to figure out all the scenarios that would make this vision not come true. Maybe if I drove the whole way—because in my vision, she was driving. I didn't know. I was scared but I was going with her.

As we were leaving the hotel, we ran into this guy named Justin, whom we had been partying with the whole trip. He was one of the racers. In fact, he was a professional driver. As we were leaving, he asked me, "Are you all right?"

He, like many of the other drivers—by now the word had spread—knew about my vision and my crazy outbreak and seemed to be really concerned.

"No," I told him the truth. "But we're going anyway."

"Why don't you take my car and I'll drive yours."

Caprice quickly told him no. But I said, "Wait a minute."

And I started thinking. In my vision, the left, back tire blows and Caprice loses control and we go over the side of a mountain and die. I didn't see Justin anywhere in that vision. I started concentrating and thinking. If he drove our car, would it happen?

"Look," he said. "If anything happens, I am better equipped to handle it. I drive for a living. I'm used to things happening and I will know what to do."

"He's right," I told Caprice, who felt that if I did really see what I saw, then she didn't want to put anyone else's life at risk. But why put ours? He was a *professional* driver. And he could handle things better than either Caprice or I. As nice as I am behind the wheel, I know that I'm not good in a situation like that. I would definitely panic and forget everything that I know—not to slam on the brakes, to turn into a spin, and all of that. I know for a fact I would bug out. And I saw what Caprice would do in that situation in my vision. But Justin could prob-ably handle it. And I didn't have a vision about him dying. I had a vision about *us* dying.

"Are you sure you want to do this?" I asked him.

"Yeah. Take my car and give me your keys."

He handed over the keys to his BMW and we gave him the keys to the Porsche. It was settled. His BMW was a stick shift, which was cool. And what was even cooler was that his wheel was on the left side. We had not only been driving on the wrong side of the road, but the wheel of the Porsche was where the passenger usually sits. It took me a couple of days to get used to that. But in Justin's BMW, I felt right at home.

Now this whole thing with Justin was a complete coin-cidence. What were the chances of one of the best racers still being at the hotel at that hour when all of the others had left? What were the chances of running into him as we were leaving? And what were the chances of him actually offering his car? I didn't care. I was just happy. And when I got behind the wheel of his car, all of my butterflies and nerves, all of my panic and fear, were gone. Caprice kept asking, "How're you feeling? What do you see? Do you sense anything?" Every hour she was asking me that, partly to be funny, but also because she wanted to know if I had any more visions. I didn't. It was all clear.

We arrived in Monaco in record time. We got to the hotel and got ready to go over to the yacht for the huge end-of-the-race party. Before we left, we had given Justin our number and taken his and asked him to call us when he got to the hotel. We had been there an hour and hadn't heard from him. I was taking forever to get dressed. So Caprice left me to go to the yacht. I was cool with that because I don't like to be rushed to get ready, anyway.

About an hour after Caprice left, she burst back into the

hotel room. I was still not ready. Caprice was hysterical and red in the face.

"Pep! Pep! Sit down!" she said, out of breath.

"What?!"

"I've got to tell you something. You're not going to believe this."

"What?" I'm thinking she met some cute guy on the yacht or something.

"Justin just called me! And guess what? The tire blew out—the left, back tire! He was coming through a tunnel right by a cliff. The car swerved and he ended up inches away from the edge of the cliff."

Throughout Europe, they have these winding roads, similar to areas in California. These roads are high in the mountains and there are no guardrails, no protection, no nothing. You mess up and slide near one of those suckers and you're a goner. Well, that tire blew out as he was coming out of the tunnel, and he spun out and lost control of the car and nearly went over. But because of his driving skills, he knew how to turn out of that spin and didn't go over.

"He said that there was no way we would have been able to handle that blowout," Caprice continued. "He said there was no way! Pep, it happened just like you said!"

I sat there for a minute both relieved and scared to death. What if Justin had not been in the lobby earlier that morning? What if he hadn't suggested we switch cars? I could be dead right now! But I was relieved. And happy to be alive and happy that Justin was alive. It was time to party. I put the finishing touches on my face and headed for the yacht.

When I got to the bar, most of the guys were there—the ones who had been telling me, "Oh, stop worrying, it's only one more day!" By this time Justin's story had circulated, and everyone knew that I wasn't crazy. They were all coming up to me, trying to talk to me, trying to get me to tell them stuff about them, asking if I had any visions for them.

"If you tell me to jump off this ship, I will do it right now," one of the guys said. "I am listening to you!"

Caprice called her mother and told her what happened. She was pissed and happy. "You better listen to Pepa from now on!" she told Caprice.

I debated telling my mother what happened. I called her to check on my kids, and she said she had the strangest dream the night before. She said she woke up crying. She had a disturbing feeling. I never told her I was going to Europe to be in a race where I would be driving two hundred miles an hour through mountains. I just said I was hanging out with Caprice because I didn't want my mother to worry. But she kept asking me if I was okay.

"I had this dream," she kept saying. I ended up telling her.

Caprice apologized and she said she would never go against me again. That story became a legend throughout Europe. And that's like our drinking story that we tell whenever we're together. After that adventure, Caprice and I became almost legendary throughout Europe. We were approached by a network in the UK to do a reality show. I was looking forward to it.

But right before we signed the deal, I got a call from Cheryl.

CHAPTER NINETEEN

Salt-N-Pepa's Here Again!

THE PHONE RANG. I WAS in my town house in Morris County lying on the bed. Frenchi (with a heart over the *i*), my little poochie, and I were relaxing. This was the last call I was expecting, but one that I desperately needed.

"Hey, girl, whatcha doing?" It was Cheryl! I hadn't heard from her in a while. We had talked a couple of times since the "I don't want to be joined at your hip" talk a few years back. But that was mostly formalities—things with the kids, a birthday greeting here and there, some work opportunities. We hadn't really talked as friends since that because, quite frankly, we weren't. I was so bitter and so angry . . . still. But something in her voice lightened my mood.

"I'm just chilling here with Frenchi, why?"

"Well, this opportunity came up. What do you think about doing a reality show?"

What?! I had to look at the phone to make sure I wasn't dreaming. "You mean, me and you? Together?"

"Yeah. I think it might be fun. There's this production company and an opportunity to do something, and we will have complete control over the whole thing."

Music to my ears. After my experiences on *The Surreal Life* and *Fame Games,* I knew how important it would be to have control. The one thing I hated was how they could cut up the tape to make you look any kind of way they wanted. You signed a waiver giving them permission to use your image and likeness and words in any way they wanted. They could leave out things you wanted in. They could edit the tape to make you look bad or good. Based on the editing, they could create drama where there was no drama and make people look crazy who weren't. That's why I shut it down and kept quiet. But to be able to do something like this *and* have control, I was interested. But I had to be sure she was serious because she had let me down before.

For the past few years I had been checking in with Cheryl to do a bunch of things—including a sitcom. Shakim had set up a meeting for us, and Cheryl agreed to fly out to Los Angeles and meet with these big-time agents. They were all excited about doing a treatment based on our lives. She told them that she would get back to them in a couple of months. I could tell from their faces that they weren't feeling that. And that deal died. I had little hope that there would ever be another opportunity for Cheryl and me to work together again. Then I got that call.

I was shocked, though. Cheryl is Miss Private and I couldn't imagine her wanting to do a show where cameras followed her around all the time.

While I wanted to do this, again I didn't trust it. I was still bitter and angry because I felt as if she had had motives when she left me for dead. And when I was talking to her about doing this reality show, I was thinking the whole time, *What's her motive now?* I know she had an album that didn't work. And I also know that you can't promote an album unless you're out there, so maybe this was her chance to get her record going again. Maybe she had tried to do things as Salt and nobody wanted just Salt, just as nobody wanted just Pep, so she had to come back and work with me. I didn't know so I was skeptical. And I had another offer with Caprice in the UK to consider.

Cheryl pushed the issue and I decided to go with it. We met with folks from the production company, Left/Right, and we set out to shoot a pilot.

Before we even shot one scene, Cheryl and I had a major blowout in the office of our then manager. The production team was interviewing us, trying to map out what the story would be for the pilot, and someone asked a question and I just let Cheryl have it.

"You were so selfish!" I started, and by the time I was finished she was in tears.

I said things that I had been thinking about and stewing over for so many years—even before she'd left the group. I had so much on my chest that it was amazing to be able to just release it all like that. But when I saw her crying, I felt bad. I couldn't keep it going. I didn't want to hurt her anymore.

In all the years we had known each other, we had never had a moment like that. We had never had a confrontation with one another. We had little fights here and there, but never a soul-baring, here's-how-I-really-feel-about-you moment. Not until that day. The production company was pissed because none of this was caught on camera. We tried to re-create it, but nothing was like that day.

I am grateful that I decided to do *The Salt-N-Pepa Show* with Cheryl. For one, I got to take a long, hard look at myself and make some changes—such as getting my nose tweaked. Seriously, I got to do some work on my insides and change a few things that weren't cute about how I was.

It gave us an opportunity to talk—to really talk—as adults and to resolve a lot of our issues. More than a chance to come back together to do something, that show gave us an opportunity to reclaim our friendship. It was a journey and the first time we came face-to-face to express ourselves. This show did amazing things for me. I fixed some things that I didn't like about myself that I could only see after I'd watched a few episodes. And it gave Cheryl and me a chance to heal and understand one another for the first time.

I discovered that Cheryl's motive for doing the show was to get back our friendship. She missed me. She missed us. And she was willing to sacrifice her comfort and her privacy to get us back to talking.

Cheryl was having a hard time once the show got picked up by VH-1. She was so nervous taping the first few shows, and I found myself feeling good about that. For one of the first times in our relationship I was in the power position. I was the reality-TV pro and knew more than she did. But instead of feeling good about it, I wanted to help her through it. Instead of wanting her to suffer and sweat, I wanted to make the process easier.

Even though I was still mad and felt I had the upper hand, I didn't want to use it. I felt sorry for her, and I didn't think I would. I didn't want to fight with her anymore. I had all of these things I wanted to say to her, and I got to say them, and I also got to see her side, which I wasn't trying to see before. We finally came to an understanding about each other. And it allowed us to come back together this time as equals, working together as a team.

It was the VH-1 *Hip-Hop Honors* and we were one of the honorees—the first females to be given these sort of props for being pioneers in the game. Queen Latifah introduced us by talking about the first time she heard us on the radio and how it inspired her to know what she could do as a woman in rap and in life. Cheryl and I were backstage. I was nervous. I am always nervous right before a show, but this time was different. Cheryl and I hadn't performed together in years. A lot of bad blood was still between us, but we had to put it all away for this.

We were to perform "Whatta Man." What was ironic about this particular performance was that En Vogue, who had also broken up, were there—all of them—to perform it with us. I remembered how they almost weren't even asked to do that song with us in the first place. Hurby, Cheryl, and I were sitting around debating who should sing the hook for this hot-ass song he had done. Several female groups were out at the time, but the hottest was En Vogue. So I said, "Let's ask them."

Hurby looked at me sideways. "En Vogue? They will never do it. They're too big. Let's shoot for—"

"Look, let's just try," I said. "Get in touch with them. All they can say is no."

Management reached out, and En Vogue not only wanted to do it, they were huge fans of Salt-N-Pepa. They were so gracious and excited. And when we came together to do the video, it was one of the best experiences we ever had working with another group. Not only were they professionals, they were all nice, too.

We had never done this song live together. We did the video, but our schedules never matched up for either of us to do it on tour with the other. So this was special.

Even Hurby showed up. He flew all the way from Haiti, where he was living, to be here on this night to pay tribute to us. Seeing him was also bittersweet. With all that we had been through, I could finally appreciate him and what he was able to accomplish. A big part of me missed Hurby, and I could tell that he missed us, too.

After the show he came backstage and congratulated us. He spent a few minutes talking to Cheryl, then he came over to me and said, "Sandra, you look good."

He never called me anything but Sandra. He never called me Pep or Sandy, it was always Sandra. He was always proper like that. Not having Hurby around made me appreciate him and what he was trying to do with us. I understood that he had a vision for this group and wanted us to live up to all of it. I knew he wanted us to be successful, and we were. A great deal of that success had to do with him.

He was like Berry Gordy putting together the Supremes. He was the driving force, especially early on, and I can look back and appreciate what he did. But he needed to learn that at some point we grow up and you have to let people grow and change and you have to let go.

At that performance we let go of a lot—a lot of bitterness, a lot of bad memories, and a lot of mistakes. That performance opened the door for us to come back together, not just as performers or a group, but also as friends. It gave Cheryl confidence to pick up the phone that day and see if we could work together again and to see if we could be friends.

When we started out, we were friends. We were these two

girls—Sandy and Cheryl—from Queens, who went to school and worked at Sears. We went from that to becoming rappers who became superstars.

Today we are working together again. We are back in the studio making music. We are writing books together (look out for our children's series). But more than that, we have found our way back to being just two girls from Queens.

We found our way back to being Sandy and Cheryl, friends!

CHAPTER TWENTY

Blacks' Magic? God's Gift!

I NEVER WANTED TO HAVE these gifts. In fact, I spent a lot of time running away from them. It's scary to see spirits and to have visions, then see them play out just as you saw them. It's scary to know things about people and not be sure if you should tell them because you don't want to scare them.

I'm learning about that. Sometimes I feel that I have to prove myself, so I want to show people who don't believe. I was recently in a Bible study group at the Christian Cultural Center in Brooklyn with the pastor, A. R. Bernard. Cheryl was there with Gavin, and midway through the study, Pastor Bernard leaned over and whispered something in Gavin's ear. Cheryl was sitting close enough to hear him, and I was on the other side of Cheryl.

"Did he just ask Gavin for a quarter?" I leaned over and asked Cheryl.

She looked at me puzzled, as if to say, *How did you know that?* But she just said, "Yes. You are always doing that!"

Cheryl probably has more stories than anyone else of my little thing popping up. Hanging with me, she has seen just about everything. She's kind of used to it by now. I don't know how or why, but things like that just come to me.

Pastor Bernard needed the quarter for a demonstration on how we perceive things from far away—it was an exercise in reality and knowing that they're two sides to a situation. He stood at the back of the church far away from everyone and said, "Do you know what's in my hand?"

I was tempted to yell, *A quarter!* Because I knew. But I thought, *Sandy, don't be such a show-off.*

It's hard not to be because so many times people just don't believe you. When I first got with Brad, he didn't allow me to even talk about my gifts.

"I don't want to hear about that shit!" he said. "Ain't none of that real."

Well, one night we were at his aunt's place in East Orange, sleeping. And I woke up and saw this light. The light formed into this figure. I could see the face so clearly, and it was scary and evil. My mother, who also has a gift, always used to say when you see something like that, you have to curse and tell it to go. So I started cursing at it.

"Get out of here!" I said, trying to whisper so I wouldn't wake Brad. "Go! Get the fuck away from him!"

Brad started choking and gurgling and trying to scream my name, but I could tell that he couldn't breathe and this figure was hovering over him.

"Get away from him!" I said again. "Leave now!"

And in a flash it was gone. Brad sat straight up in bed and started gasping for air. He'd seen the figure and knew that it was choking him. He was a believer from that moment on. We had to move downstairs and sleep on his aunt's couch, and he built some sort of altar with candles in his room to supposedly ward off evil. After that experience he would tell people, "Yo, ask Sandy anything you need to know; she knows stuff for real!"

I often debate whether I should tell people, especially when I see illnesses or worse. It's tough. You don't ever want to be the bearer of bad news. But sometimes you can save a life. A man lived around my way named Mr. Simmons. I had a vision about him that something was wrong with his liver. After a couple of days, I decided to tell him.

"Ain't nothing wrong with my liver," he told me. "I feel fine. And I don't drink."

"Please, Mr. Simmons, just get your liver checked out," I told him.

He went to the doctor and they ended up admitting him to the hospital, where he stayed for a month. He had some rare liver condition. And it had nothing to do with drinking.

I told my niece Georgia about her husband, Danny, after I had a vision that something was wrong with his blood cells. Now I don't get specific terms in my visions. I just see liver problems or, in this case, blood cell problems. Danny went to get it checked out and found out he was diabetic and had some issues with his blood cells.

I had a vision, a dream, about Malik Sealy, who was a basketball star at St. John's University and who was playing for the Minnesota Timberwolves at the time, the night he died. I woke up in a cold sweat and told Brad what I had seen. I didn't know

Malik. I had met him one time at a party through a friend. So I kept asking myself why was I dreaming about him. In my dream he was in a bad car accident. I could see the truck that hit him, and I could see his SUV clearly, the color and everything.

I saw him reaching down to change a CD and that's when it happened. I turned on the television and there was no news about it. I checked the papers, nothing. I called my sister who lived in Minnesota to see if she could find out something. Again, I didn't know Malik or anyone whom I could call to find out. The next day, my brother-in-law called, and sure enough it was the front-page story there, and they had a picture of the SUV and the color, and it was just as I'd described. They didn't have in the article about his changing a CD because there was no way that they could have known that.

His spirit stayed on me. He wanted me to tell his wife, Lisa, that he was at peace and that he was okay. I didn't want to do it. I mean, how was going to track her down and say, "Hello, you don't know me, but I'm Pepa from Salt-N-Pepa, and your husband's spirit came to me in a vision and he wants you to know that he's okay?"

No way in the world was I going to do that. So I didn't. But I kept bumping into people who knew his wife, and his name kept coming up in conversations out of the blue and so did his wife's name. But I still couldn't do it. I just couldn't do it.

So if Lisa is reading this, Malik wanted you to know that he's okay. He's at peace. He is complete. And he has no regrets.

I was haunted by another celebrity spirit for years. Aaliyah. Again, I had met her in passing at industry functions, but I didn't know her personally. But she came to me frequently in a dream.

Miss Thing (I call her that because she's so fierce) started coming to me frequently, and she always came the same way: suspended in midair. Her face was blackened, as if she was burned, and she was sad. I could feel the sadness. She was wearing this beautiful, flowing, white draping that just hung around her body like a cloud.

This vision haunted me for about a year before I finally got some closure. I hate a vision that I can't figure out or that doesn't come to a conclusion. This one was really bothering me. I didn't know Aaliyah, I didn't know her family, and I had no way of really asking anyone about it without looking completely crazy. She kept coming to me. And I kept asking, *Why me?!* I wasn't close to her, why was she coming to me?

One day, I was at a party. A friend of mine was hosting a night at a club uptown in Harlem. She was throwing a party for Misa Hylton-Brim, who is a stylist and also the mother of Puffy's son Justin. I was there enjoying myself when Misa and Missy and a bunch of other people came in. I was introduced to them and I left shortly after. I later found out that this day was Aaliyah's birthday.

The next day I got a call from a friend who said that Missy was asking for my number. She was working on an album and was a huge Salt-N-Pepa fan and wanted me to be on one of her songs. I was flattered. At this point I had pretty much given up any hopes of ever recording again. We didn't end up recording but we became friends. One night we were talking and Aaliyah came up in conversation. She and Missy were close, and her death was still affecting Missy.

She told me that before Aaliyah died she had told Missy about a dream she was having. In this dream her face was blackened and she was suspended in midair, wearing this white, flowing garment. When I heard that, I dropped on the floor and rolled around. I couldn't believe it. That was my exact vision. And then it all came together and made sense. I didn't know what Aaliyah was trying to tell me, but after Missy shared that with me I knew why Aaliyah was sad. She wanted to send a message to her family to stop grieving and move on. She wanted them to stop doing the things they were doing. She wanted them to be happy and know that she can't rest until they do move on. Her sadness was because she couldn't have any peace. That she couldn't rest as long as there was turmoil in her family.

I know a lot of people have these visions. I have talked with John Edward and I know about Sylvia Browne and people like that. But for me, I still feel uncomfortable talking about it because it does seem weird and strange. But I also know I have helped people. I have given comfort or actually saved a life.

Most of my visions are about other people, though. I wish I had more visions about myself. I probably wouldn't have ended up in so many of the situations that I ended up in. I often ask, "Now why didn't you see that one coming?!" Where are my powers when I really need them?

Every now and then, though, I will get a vision that spares me, such as during the Gumball Rally when I saw that Caprice and I were going to go over a cliff, or in the Forty Projects in Queens with my friend Sonya when we were being set up for a gang rape.

When my voice tells me to do something, I do it. At times it has told me to leave a club, and I have, and I've found out later about a shoot-out there.

I know a lot of people have visions and feelings and probably think they're crazy. I know I thought so for a long time. Cheryl and I have had discussions about whether this thing that I have is from God. I know I don't go to church as often as I'd like, but I believe in and know God, and I know that what I have is directly from him. I know it's a gift. So I don't play with it. I feel blessed and thankful to have it. And I don't change a dime.

CHAPTER TWENTY-ONE

Celibacy: Very Necessary!

IT WAS OCTOBER 2005; I was single and just out there wilding. I had been through so much drama with the men in my life, so much strife and stress, that now I decided that I was just going to chill and date and have fun. In my entire life, I had never just dated. If I went out with you and I liked you, I had to be in a relationship.

I was never the kind of girl who had one-night stands. If I slept with you, you were going to be my man. I had this fantasy of having it the way people were supposed to have it—with a man loving me and treating me well. And me being devoted to him. Well, I got the devotion part down. I never cheated on any of my guys. Never.

I didn't cheat partly because I never thought I could get away with it. I never understood how industry people could be stepping out on their man or woman and not think that it would get back. I knew someone would recognize me and run back and say, "I saw Pepa at Tony Roma's or Red Lobster with so and so." So I never cheated. But also, I never *wanted* to cheat. I wanted to hold it down like that for my man because that's what I wanted from him. I wanted it to be just him and me forever.

But that never happened. So being single again, I decided, "Why not?" Let me just date and have fun.

I was hanging out with this guy. He was sexy as hell and I was really feeling him. We had known each other for a few years but never got into anything. We were hanging out and somehow ended up back at my place. We were kissing and getting into it, and all of sudden I got nauseated. I tried to fight through it because I really wanted him, but I had to stop. I excused myself and went to the bathroom. I splashed some water on my face and looked in the mirror.

"What the fuck?" I was talking to myself. I pulled it together and went back. We started back up and I got grossed out. I mean, if we didn't stop, I would have thrown up on him.

"What's the matter?" he asked me.

"Um, I don't know. I'm not feeling well. Maybe I'm tired."

But I wasn't tired. Something else was going on inside me. I don't know if it was spiritual or what, but I couldn't sleep with him. I had lost my appetite completely, and the thought of making love to him was making me sick. Believe me, it wasn't him. I mean, we were practically naked and his body was ridiculous, just ridiculous. He was making all the right moves, pushing all the right buttons, and I just couldn't do it.

At first, I thought maybe it was something I ate. But it wasn't. And there definitely wasn't anything wrong with him. I knew that I didn't want to sleep with *anyone*. It was as if my body was rebelling against a lifetime of bad decisions.

My mom used to tease me about my men: "No more man frames for you!"

She called the men I had been with "man frames" because they were just window dressing or empty inside. They were a shell of a man, not real men. I didn't see it then. But my mother was right. And no disrespect to the men. It was me; it was my fault. I allowed them to be less than a man with me. I allowed them to do the things that they did to me because I didn't love myself enough to stop them. I can't blame them entirely. I have to blame me.

I remember when I was going through all of that drama saying to myself, *How long are you going to keep doing this?* I had a daughter. What kind of example was I setting for her? I had a son, who was getting older and starting to understand things, starting to see Mommy with a black eye here and a busted lip there. What kind of message was I sending him?

Fans would constantly come up to me and tell me how much they loved me.

"You empower me!" one of them told me.

"Girl, you are so strong!" another said. "You inspire me."

I felt like a fraud. I was projecting this one image and at the same time I would be walking around with shades to hide black eyes. But that's typical. I always gave good advice, but I just wasn't following it. I would tell Cheryl, "You know you deserve better. You don't have to put up with that shit from Hurby." Meanwhile, I was allowing all kinds of things to happen to me.

I was always there with a Pep talk for whoever was listening. I just tuned my own self out. I needed to walk the walk.

It went from getting physically ill when I tried to have sex to making a decision to not even try. I was going to swear off men, after all these years. Go cold turkey. Just quit. It seemed that all of my problems revolved around men—even when it wasn't my fault. Even when I wasn't directly involved.

One example of this was in 1994. I ended up in one of those *National Enquirer* type of magazines under a headline: "Is Pepa a Home Wrecker?" Remember the night Lisa (Left Eye) Lopes burned down the house of Andre Rison (former Atlanta Falcons wide receiver)? Well, I was sort of in the middle of that.

Andre and I never messed around. I'm innocent of that crime. I am so innocent. But I did know him and we were really cool. Salt-N-Pepa used to do a lot of NFL spots for *Monday Night Football*. And we would do some NFL parties. I met Andre at one of those parties and we hit it off. We went bowling and were bugging out and laughing. I would bump into from time to time at different clubs. And that was it.

He told me later how everything went down. Apparently he had been talking about me to her. Telling her how cool I was. Brothers, you can't do that. Your girl will immediately be suspicious. Now, maybe he did like me like that, but again, we never went there. One night, he and Lisa are watching TV and my video comes on, and he gets all excited and says something like "Pep, that my girl!"

Maybe she was feeling that he was trying to holler at me and she didn't like it. That very night, we had a concert at the Fox Theatre in Atlanta, and Andre and Lisa came to the show. I got them backstage tickets and the whole nine.

After the show, I was backstage and I left my dressing room for something. At the same time, Andre was nowhere to be found. Lisa came into my dressing room looking for him, and when she didn't see me and couldn't find him, she jumped to conclusions. She assumed that we were together. This is what he told me. She finally found him and they went home and argued that whole night. He told me he couldn't take it anymore and left. When he did, that's when the teddy bears and the sneakers went in the Jacuzzi with the lighter fluid and the whole house got burned to the ground.

That was a huge story. And the tabloids had started getting wind of what had happened. Lisa talked about him cheating, but no one knew the whole story or the truth. Then I end up in this tabloid in a picture from the "Shoop" video with that headline: "Is Pepa a Home Wrecker?" TLC was a big group. And Salt-N-Pepa was huge, too. And you add in an NFL star and a burned-down mansion and you have the makings of a real scandal. It was about to be on. That story was going to catch fire like Andre's house. I was saved, though. That same week O. J. Simpson decided to kill his wife and her friend in California. And nobody cared about Andre Rison, Lisa (Left Eye) Lopes, and me. Thank you, O.J.!

But that incident showed me how crazy we women can get over a man. I was Lisa. I have been on that side of it with Ta-Ta and even Brad. I would be out and see Brad talking to an ugly girl and her pretty friend would be nearby, and I knew the deal. The ugly friend was giving her friend's number to Brad, and I would break on him and go crazy. But that's what it was, crazy.

I know how that feels and I never want to feel that way again about anyone. That's not love.

And most of that craziness comes from not loving yourself. Because if you love yourself, you wouldn't do things so destructive to yourself over a man. If he's cheating on you, then you have to love yourself enough to keep it moving, no matter how much it hurts. Don't burn up his stuff. Leave. Don't curse him out, leave. If he's disrespecting you, you have to respect yourself enough to walk away from that.

On October 23, 2005, just a few weeks before my birthday, I decided to walk away from all that. I decided to shut it completely down and be celibate. It was time. I had to learn how to love myself. And I had to be that woman that could attract that man who would deserve to be with me.

The way people go on these fasts to cleanse their bodies of toxins, I decided to fast from sex, to clean my spirit from another kind of toxin.

True love? To tell you the truth, I have no idea what that really is. But I want to find out. As you know by now, I haven't had much luck in that area. I decided not to have sex until I found love—real love. I figured that I had done just about everything else, so I might as well try something different. And I'm not settling for anything close, or anything that looks like love. I want the whole shebang. I deserve it all!

And, no, I'm not necessarily saving it for marriage. I still believe in marriage and I would love to be married again—to the right man. But I'm not necessarily waiting for marriage to be with someone. What I'm waiting for is someone special enough to give it to. I want to be in love—true love. No one seems to care about love anymore. I want to bring it back to the old school. I should be something that a man is willing to work for. Shouldn't we feel that special, special enough for someone to wait to have it?

I have been on the not-so-special side too often. I have given myself away for cheap too many times. I can remember sitting there at dinner thinking, *What will I have to do for all of this?* As if I didn't deserve a free meal!

How do you lose yourself as a woman? It starts with the

little things—allowing him to talk to you a certain way. Then it progresses from there. I've allowed a lot. I've done everything from allowing a man to beat me to signing for a loan for a car to paying his cell phone bill. I can't tell you how many cars I've been stuck with and insurance and all that when the relationship is over. A man who will let a woman do that doesn't love her. How can you love someone if you ruin her credit and put her in debt?

Another thing to watch out for is a man who tries to keep a woman from her friends and family. That's a clear sign. If he is pulling you away from people who love you, who care about you, who will look out for you, he doesn't love you. Why would a man want you away from that?

I know now what it looks like when a man doesn't love you. I am working on what love does look like.

I realized just recently that what I was searching for was my father. I used to call my man "Daddy," and stuff like that. So I attracted men who were controlling, who liked that I was weak. They didn't see any strength in me and liked that I didn't stand up for myself. A real man isn't threatened by a strong woman.

I used to answer to my guys. If I was on the phone and my man told me to get off, I would. If I was going out and he told me to be back by eleven, I was back by eleven. That's how I became a victim. That went on for a long time—too long—before I finally said, "What the hell!"

Enough!

It's hard for a lot of people to believe that I am celibate because I am so wild. But who said that you have to stop having fun just because you're not having sex? As a matter of fact, I have more fun now than I did when I was in relationships. I can dance and drink and party all night and do whatever I want, and

I know that I don't have to answer to anyone. Also, if I'm hanging out with a man, I'm honest. I tell him up front that he's not getting any. You get to really know a person when sex is not an option. Men can be themselves when they aren't working to get into your panties. The pressure is off them, too.

Now when I date, I turn into a reporter. I turn into Gary Sheffield. I am interviewing to see if this man is right for me. I want to know everything about a guy. I don't want any more surprises. I realized that even though I thought I knew all my boyfriends and husbands, I was actually sleeping with strangers.

The next man I get with, I want to know him. You can't know somebody in a couple of weeks, or a couple of months even. So why are you sleeping with him that quickly? Everyone is on his best behavior those first few months when everything is nice. When I first met Brad and we were out and he accidentally stepped on my foot, he said, "Ooh, baby, I'm sorry I stepped on your foot." Two years in and he stepped on my foot he said, "Bitch, your foot was in the way!"

I want courtship. I want that old-school mentality of dating and getting to know someone. You have to give it some time to see who it is you're really dealing with. And he will show you . . . in time. That's why I'm saving it. I'm waiting. This time, I am going to take my time.

CHAPTER TWENTY-TWO

Do You Want Me?
This Is What You Have to Do

I BELIEVE IN WRITING THINGS down, making a plan, and following it. I used to do this for most things in my life. I did it for everything except for the kind of man I wanted. I recently put together a list, a kind of blueprint for the kind of man I am looking for. And if he wants to be with me, he's going to have to fit all of the categories—not a couple or some, but all.

No more compromising. No more lowering my standards. It's all or nothing. I have waited this long, I might as well hold out until I get everything I need.

Here are the must-haves on my checklist for the next man in my life:

1. He must be spiritual.

If he doesn't believe in God, I can't believe in him. I'm not messing with the devil anymore. I have already been there, done that, and it didn't work for me. I am heading down a spiritual path in my life, and I need my next man to be walking down that path alongside me.

2. He has to have his own ish.

I've taken care of every man I have ever been with in one form or another—whether it was emotionally or financially. I was the breadwinner. The head of the house. I had the house, I bought the cars. And in many cases, I ended up losing most everything.

   I want my next man to have his own stuff—his own money, house, and car. I'm not saying I want him to take care of me. I just want him to have as much to lose in the relationship as I do.

3. He has to have as much or more to lose than I do.

I have a career. I want my next man to have a career. I don't want his career to be about following my career. I want him to have a business or I want his career to be as big or bigger than mine. When people have nothing to lose, then they may have no problem taking you down. I'm not getting involved with a man with nothing to lose.

   This is similar to his having his own stuff. But it's deeper. Because a man who has something to lose will think about what he will do before he does it. I want a man who thinks first, then acts.

4. He has to be honest—about his feelings and everything else.

They say the truth will set you free. I cannot and will not deal with a lying man. I need to be able to trust him completely—even if I don't like what he's saying.

I'm looking for love, and if you're coming into my world and you say you're looking for love, then let that be the truth. I can respect a guy who says, "I'm not ready and this is not something that I think I can do." Thank you! I appreciate that. Then I can move on.

I want a man who is truthful about his feelings, who understands what he's feeling. I want a man who knows what it means to love. To me, love is the desire to benefit the other person and a willingness to sacrifice yourself for that person. And it has to be mutual. It has to go both ways. If one is doing it and the other isn't, it's not going work.

5. I want the next man to be the *man* in the relationship.

I want my man to take charge. I want him to tell me that he's taking me to dinner, and I want him to make the reservations. I want him to surprise me with a trip to somewhere exotic and come home and tell me, "Baby, pack your bags. We're going . . . ," instead of putting me on the phone with the travel agent to plan.

I want him to bring me flowers, as that movie says, just because it's Wednesday. I don't want flowers just on Valentine's Day or my birthday. I want a man who is thoughtful enough to do things like that just because. It's the simple things that matter. And being a man is not about being macho; it's about doing the little things, taking the lead when you're supposed to, and doing the things that make me happy.

6. He has to know that chivalry is not dead!
Please hold a door open for me and pull out my chair when I go to sit down. Wait for me to get into the car first. As a matter of fact, walk around and open my car door and wait for me to get in. And don't do it just because it's the first date. Do it for the rest of our lives together because I deserve that.

7. He has to be healthy.
I'm no longer into what a man looks like physically. (Don't get me wrong, if he's cute, that's a plus. But it's not the most important thing.) I figure if he's a little overweight, we can work out together and take care of that. But I want my next man to be health conscious and healthy. I want him to care about himself. Because I want him to be around for the duration. I want someone to grow old with me, and he can't do that if he's dropping dead from a heart attack as soon I get with him. (And because I'm waiting for this Mr. Right, he better know that when I do get with him, I'm going to be really bringing it. So he had better be in some kind of shape.)

This checklist is a reminder for me to demand what I want. To get what I'm worth. You know how you give a job referral? Can you refer your man to another woman? Be honest. Can you tell another woman that the man you're with is worth being with? If you say no, then he's not worth being with you.

When you have an investment, you want your money to

grow. If you're banker tells you that you're losing money, you will pull your money out. It's the same thing in a relationship. Is it growing? If it's not, you have to go.

Make a list of the things you want from the man you're with. Don't settle for anything less. And if you find yourself in a relationship and he stops living up to your list, then it might be time for you to leave. You only have one life on this earth. You should spend it happy and being treated with respect. But the only way that's going to happen is for you to demand it.

CHAPTER TWENTY-THREE

Pep Talk

WHEN I STARTED WORKING ON this book, I had a lot of things bottled up inside. There were things that I still didn't want to talk about and things I didn't even want to face. It took a minute, but I eventually opened up and I ended up sharing things here that I've never told anyone—not even my family.

It seems like everyone has a book out nowadays. And it seems as if everyone is telling it *all*. This was not a tell-all. I know some of you are saying, "Well, damn, there's more to tell?" Yes. There were many things I didn't feel the need to tell. Because this wasn't about exposing everything, this book was my chance to heal.

This was my therapy—to get off my chest some of the things that I feel had stopped me from growing into the woman I was supposed to be. For too many years I walked around with a smile on face, I was always joking and partying. I was the fun girl. But I had so much going on inside that was far from fun. There were things that I figured I could just laugh off or cover up with a smile or by having fun at a party.

If I ignored it, maybe those feelings would just go away. Well, they didn't go away. And what I learned through this process was that things are a whole lot better when you get them out in the open.

In the entertainment industry, everything is about appearances and how things look. People spend a lot of money to have the right image. But artists, celebrities, entertainers, are all human beings. We all have issues and a past, just like everybody else.

I learned that doing this book, too. Not that I didn't know they were all human, but in talking about some of the things in this book to some of my friends in the business, I realized how many of them had been through some of the same things—from the molestation to the abuse. My situation wasn't so unique.

I started writing this book for me. I was angry and bitter when I started it. I was mad at myself for constantly choosing the wrong men. I was mad at Cheryl for leaving the group and taking away my career. I was mad at the world. But I stopped being mad and started to see that every single thing that I went through—especially the bad stuff—ended up being a blessing. Because I survived it. And it made me stronger. But more than all of that, it put me in a place where my stories could help other people.

When I finished doing this book, I realized that I hadn't done it just for me at all. This book might be able to help some women get through their issues. It might get some teenager out there to not give up and keep pushing forward because I did. If I could go through all of this shit and come out of it, then so can you.

As long as you have breath in your body, you have the power to make a change in your life for the better. It's not just going to happen. You have to actually do something to make it happen.

I didn't stay mad and sit in my anger and my bad feelings. I didn't just sit on my ass and wait for time to pass me by. I kept it moving. I had some fun. I even did a few reality shows. And that attitude prepared me for the next phase in my life. I never expected Cheryl to want to work together again. But when she did make that call, I was ready. In fact, when we were doing our own reality show, I was the one helping her through it because I was a pro at it by then. That was a real switch.

And because I didn't just sit still and wallow in self-pity, I was also open to work with her and try and heal our relationship. And I can honestly say, that our relationship today is more honest and more real than it has ever been. We're both in a different place in our lives. And while we're still complete opposites, we also still go together like salt and pepper. We're still sisters.

As far as my relationships with men: Taking this break and being celibate for these years was maybe the biggest eye-opener I have ever had. I learned that I *can* be by myself. And being alone doesn't mean that I'm lonely. It just means that I appreciate me. This time has giving me the space for the first time in my life to find out who I really am and what I'm really about. During this time, I have found out that I really like myself. And I can't turn back—not for any man, not for anyone.

Now don't get me wrong, I do miss having a man around, if you know what I mean. And I do get lonely sometimes. And it is very hard. I have to fast forward through some of the love scenes in my soap operas because it reminds me of what I'm missing out on. I know there are a lot of women who have chosen to be celibate and some of them act like it's a piece of cake. Well, I'm here to tell you that's it's not a piece of cake for me. I struggle with it sometimes.

But what keeps me going is knowing that I don't want to go back. I haven't worked this hard for all of these years to mess it all up. I know that even if I feel empty and alone today, it's for a good reason. I know that the reward will be so fulfilling.

I'm not going to cheat myself out of my reward. That's how I feel about it. I know I deserve to have it all. A lot of people get anxious. They don't have faith. They get scared that maybe it won't come. But not me. I'm going to wait. I'm not settling. Not anymore. I deserve the best. No more man frames for me!

There's a proverb that I have written in my journal that I look at often. It says: A fool learns from his own mistakes. A wise man learns from the mistakes of others.

I must have made every mistake a person could make. Please don't go through all of the shit I went through to get your lesson. Learn from my mistakes.

I finally have! And I'm taking it to the next level: I'm learning from other's too.

Epilogue

by Missy Elliott

SALT-N-PEPA. I DON'T KNOW ANY female rapper who isn't a fan of Salt-N-Pepa. They are the reason why I became a rapper. As a little girl, I had never seen girls do the things they were doing. They were not only rhyming, they had the style that made you want to dress like them. They had the swagger. I was a fan from Day One.

But getting to know Pepa over these years has been more than I ever expected. I always tell her that I'm still a fan first. I tell her, "Y'all just don't know the doors you opened up." There were a lot of female rappers, but Salt-N-Pepa were the ones who made it real and made it possible for most of us to even know we could get into this game.

In my home, I have pictures who inspire me and whose

shoulders I have climbed on to be where I am. I have a huge picture of Salt-N-Pepa on the wall right outside of my studio. And when I'm working, I can look at that picture and get some inspiration.

I love Pep. She knows I don't go out. I usually have people over to my house. And Pep always tells me how she used to party. Now I was thinking, can't nobody party that hard, so I challenged her. I wanted to see how much she could really drink. Fifteen shots of Patrone in a row. No lie! Pep drank them back-to-back-to-back and she didn't flinch, stumble, or mumble afterward. She didn't lean on anything or earl. When she finished those fifteen shots, she was no different that before she started. I was like, "Daaaaaaamn!" I don't know any dudes who could do that. Pep is no joke!

Pep will do just about anything. Don't dare her. I got her doing *Dance Dance Revolution*. That's my workout. She's come over in her tight jeans, tight baby tee, and her lace front wig, and we act a fool. She can last about three songs before she's done.

"Oh, no! You got me sweating out my hair!" she tells me.

One of the things I love about Pep is her spirit. She's always laughing. She even cracks herself up. She will be sitting there and say something under her breath so funny that she just gets weak laughing. And I can't help but laugh, too. I don't even know what she said or what's so funny, but I just get caught up. That's Pep. She always brings this warm energy wherever she goes.

That's why this book is so important. People need to see the other side of Pep, too. They need to see the come up. They need to see the sadness. They need to see the imperfections. A lot of times people look at celebrities as if they have perfect lives. We have the money, the fame, and we don't have any problems. It's our problems that have shaped many of us to do the things we're doing. It was our struggles that made us stronger. And these kinds of stories are universal. Celebrities go through the same things that everyday people go through.

My mother wasn't a celebrity. But she could relate to Pepa's story of being abused because she went through a similar situation, as have a lot of women. I was molested by two cousins, so I can feel where Pep is coming from on that and I can see how she handled it versus how I handled it and I can learn something from her story, too.

Hers wasn't a Cinderella story. We saw them with the fly clothes and the hit records, but there was a lot she had to overcome too, and it made her stronger as a woman.

Look at her. She's by herself and taking care of two children. She's always telling me, "I ain't got no man!" And I'm looking at a woman who doesn't need one. Don't go searching for something you don't need. Do you, until that right one comes along. This is a way to learn to love yourself.

God allows us to go through things for a reason. Maybe Pep went through so many of the things she did so the next person won't have to.

Like I said, I'm her friend. But I'm a fan first. And Pep having the courage to do this book has made me even more of a fan!